Outdoor Moments with God

Books by W. Phillip Keller:

Splendor from the Sea
As a Tree Grows
Bold under God—A Fond Look at a Frontier Preacher
A Shepherd Looks at Psalm 23
A Layman Looks at the Lord's Prayer
Rabboni—Which Is to Say, Master
A Shepherd Looks at the Good Shepherd and His Sheep
A Gardener Looks at the Fruits of the Spirit
Mighty Man of Valor—Gideon
Mountain Splendor
Taming Tension
Expendable
Still Waters
A Child Looks at Psalm 23
Ocean Glory
Walking with God
On Wilderness Trails
Elijah—Prophet of Power
Salt for Society
A Layman Looks at the Lamb of God
Lessons from a Sheep Dog
Wonder O' the Wind
Joshua—Mighty Warrior and Man of Faith
A Layman Looks at the Love of God
Sea Edge
David I
David II
Sky Edge
Chosen Vessels
In the Master's Hands
Predators in Our Pulpits
Songs of My Soul
Thank You, Father
God Is My Delight
Pleasures Forevermore
Strength of Soul
Outdoor Moments with God

Outdoor
Moments
with God

W. Phillip Keller

PUBLICATIONS

Grand Rapids, MI 49501

Outdoor Moments with God by W. Phillip Keller.

Copyright © 1994 by W. Phillip Keller.

Published by Kregel Publications, a division of Kregel, Inc., P.O. Box 2607, Grand Rapids, MI 49501. Kregel Publications provides trusted, biblical publications for Christian growth and service. Your comments and suggestions are valued.

Cover photo: Patricia Sgrignoli, POSITIVE IMAGES
Cover art, design and illustrations: Ron Bell
Book design: Alan G. Hartman

Library of Congress Cataloging-in-Publication Data
Keller, W. Phillip (Weldon Phillip), 1920-
    Outdoor moments with God / W. Phillip Keller.
        p.   cm.
    1. Nature—Religious aspects—Christianity—
Meditations. I. Title.
BT695.5.K45   1994   242—dc20   92-17859
                                                          CIP

ISBN 0-8254-2996-x

    1 2 3 4 5 6 Printing / Year 98 97 96 95 94

Printed in the United States of America

To

Al Bryant,

my longtime friend and splendid editor,

with

hearty esteem and humble thanks.

Contents

Why This Book?

The simple answer to that blunt question is that often, often outdoors, flashes of inspiration come with brilliant illumination in a matter of moments. Suddenly, swiftly, clear spiritual perception of profound truth sweeps into my own spirit like an artist's painting in vivid colors. The impression comes in an instant but endures forever.

These moving outdoor moments stir my spirit.
They parallel the parables Christ used, to convey truth.
They are lessons learned from the realm of nature.

In actual fact our Father, through the creative work of Christ and by the agency of His Spirit, has produced two remarkable books. One is His Word, articulated in human language we can comprehend. The other is His creation, the remarkable and lovely natural realm around us which can be read clearly.

Because He is the genius behind both books, the Creator and the originator of both the natural and the supernatural revelations, the principles which apply in the one also function in the other. The two realms are contiguous, and they are complimentary.

This is why when Christ spoke of eternal virtues He used such simple subjects as soil, seed, grass, trees, birds, and bread to explain supernatural truth. We call these parables: insights using natural, outdoor subjects to help us clearly grasp complex spiritual principles.

Having spent most of my life outdoors, this has been the way in which Christ has revealed Himself, His character, and His ways to me most emphatically. He has given me an enormous love for the land, the plants, the wildlife, the mountains, the ocean, the plains, and all the outdoors. My outdoor adventures have been an enduring delight in His company.

The pages that follow are an attempt to share some of those everyday moments with the reader. My earnest prayer is that the word pictures painted here will enrich your understanding of the Master and His ways with you.

Please read slowly, slowly, to relish and to reflect!

Thanksgiving

It is that season of the year; that
Season in my soul; that season in my long
Life of quiet adventures with my father, God.
To him I give hearty genuine gratitude.
To precious people who pray for me.
To Fern Webber, a joyful, diligent secretary.
To Ursula who shares life's adventures.
To Christ Himself, my companion and
Most high Majesty who makes it possible.

Tracks In The Snow

Day after day the snow fell steadily. Its fine and delicate adornment swathed the landscape in a shining lacework of sparkling sequins. It decorated the trees, smoothed over the rough contours of rocks and soil to leave the impression of pristine purity.

But it also clogged the roads, drifted in driveways, and brought a silent burden of shoveling. Soon the roar of snow plows and the scrape-scrape-scrape of snow shovels shattered the pristine silence of winter.

Again and again and again I had gone out, bundled up in heavy winter boots, warm sweaters, and lined gloves to clear the accumulation. It seemed, at times, such a heavy, strenuous chore. Or was it that my muscles and tendons were no longer up to the task?

One evening, completely exhausted, I collapsed in a tired heap on the couch. And I wondered—I wondered—I wondered to myself if I was up to a whole winter of this heavy labor.

The next day, after still more snow, I was astonished to look out and see that half the driveway was already shoveled clear. It was simply too good to really be true. Who could be so generous, so thoughtful, so kind?

Carefully I pulled on my warm winter outer wear. In quietness I went outside to walk on the bare pavement. The question kept running through my mind-racing through my emotions—stirring my spirit—*"Who would do this? Who is so selfless? Who cares this much?"*

It was a moving moment.
There was no one around—no one to ask—no clue.
Or was there? Yes, there was! It excited me!
There was a set of tracks in the snow.
Someone with very big boots had done the good deed.
The imprint of his soles was unmistakable.
And those footprints would lead me to the one with a big heart.

My old tracking skills, used for so many years to follow big game over difficult terrain, leaped into life. I would take up the trail and track down my unknown, unseen helper. Sure enough the tracks lead up the road and into a kind neighbor's home. I had found my friend. He seemed pleased and somewhat amused that I would take the trouble to discover who had moved the mountain of snow.

Grinning sheepishly he remarked, "I knew you were an old time tracker. Can't get away with much around here!"

But in the instant after that little exchange a stirring impression was suddenly etched on my spirit by the Spirit of the Most High. It was as vivid, sharp, concise as the deep boot marks I had just followed.

Tracks in the snow.
  Footprints in time.
    A clear cut trail across life.
      Where do they go—what do they show?
        Each of us leaves an imprint behind.
          Has it been to help and cheer, or. . . or . . .
          Would we rather it not be known?

But we are known!
Every twist, every turn, every tangle in our trail is under the clear scrutiny of our caring Friend . . . Christ Himself. He assures us again and again and again that He is ever here—ever near—ever to cheer.

Why, why, why then do we dodge, duck, and dart this way and that to cover our tracks? He reads them like an open book. He knows where we have been—what we have done—where we have helped. And, yes, where we might have hurt.

No need to try to hide. No point in pretending!

How much better to leave tracks in time that tell of lending a helping hand, lifting someone's load a little, bringing a bit of love and laughter into someone's dark day.

Tracks in the snow. My personal signature on a page of time.

The Little White Pine

W hen first we moved into this home, high on its hot, sunburned rock ridge, the little white pine was struggling to survive beside the driveway. Someone with a deep love for the delicate foliage of this handsome species had planted the little tree in this unpromising spot. It had struck root in the shale and sand of the hot hills, but it was far from happy in such a dry desert setting.

Normally our western white pines flourish in the cooler climate of the coast or on the higher slopes of the mountain ranges where they thrive in the moist conditions of upland forests. There they grow into grand, impressive trees. Their mighty trunks carry their proud crowns into the clouds. Their rich green boughs sway and sing in the storms of rain, snow, and mist that sweep across the slopes.

But our little white pine had none of that grandeur. It stood less than six feet tall. It stood there in the hot gravel and burning sun defying the desert heat. It was stressed to the limit just trying to stay alive.

From the first day I saw it, the soft green of its needles, the gentle contours of its shape attracted my attention. It tried so hard to be at its best in spite of so much adversity. Somehow its fortitude ignited a fierce affection for the little tree within my spirit. So I became determined to see it flourish in this formidable spot.

The first year I took great pains to prune it with loving care. All the dead twigs, broken branches, and discarded boughs were removed one by one. It was shaped carefully so that the fierce winds from the desert would not break its crown or bruise its branches.

Then I went and found another huge pine with a deep bed of needles beneath it. These I gathered up in glee and carried them to my little tree. With loving care I spread a virtual quilt of decaying needles deep around the base of the tiny tree. It would shelter the soil from wind and sun and drought.

The blanket of forest duff would keep the spreading roots cool and moist, even on the hottest days. And any moisture that fell on the ground would be preserved to refresh the sturdy tree. What was more, the extra moisture would enable the soil bacteria to break down the needles I brought in. These would decompose into rich humus, acidic in content, which white pines relish.

It looked like rough treatment. It was less precise and proper than the manicured gravel beds before. But it was precisely what the little tree needed to burst into new life. Within a couple of years its whole shape and size and sweep had changed dramatically. The long, slender branches were covered in lovely foliage. The greenery thickened into a strong, dense growth that could resist any heat. Handsome cones formed on the topmost branches. The little white pine had become my favorite tree.

Even the most ferocious gusts of wind serve only one fine purpose. They strip off the mature brown needles to deposit them as an ever increasing bounty on the bed of humus around the tree. What before was a grim little tree going nowhere has grown into a specimen of gentle beauty under the master's hands.

Often as I stand beside the tree, relishing its company, finding pure pleasure in its progress, I ask myself some profound, soul-searching questions.

Do I respond this well to the pruning, painful, cutting events my Master allows to cut across my life?

Do I resent the apparent rubbish and debris that fall from other lives and are deposited around my feet? Do I see it as so much waste and clutter? Or is it possible that this is the means by which my Lord sees fit to enrich my days, to nourish my soul? Do I respond with new growth, new godliness, new grace?

Are the sudden winds of adversity that strip away my old, clinging *self-life* a hardship or the stirring wind of His Spirit sweeping clean my spirit?

Oh, Christ, open my eyes to see!

Frozen River

I t was a mission of mercy. A dear fellow had simply decided to leave his home, his wife, his cherished memories in an act of coldhearted abandonment. Why or how or what prompted this drastic family fracture only our Father fully understood.

But I was off in search of this lost and wandering soul. All I had to guide me was a scribbled address on a scrap of paper where he might be found. It was in a northern town, a tough town with a rough reputation. But at least it was a slim clue.

Even though it was some 150 miles away across the high cattle country, already deeply blanketed with snow, I was prepared to go. What if early winter had settled in? What if the roads were icy, drifted in, and dangerous to drive? Still, I would head out to search for this tragic man so far astray from his family, from his friends, from his Father above.

Did not Christ urge us to go out into the highways and byways and compel the wanderers to come into His care?

I left at dawn. The first half of the drive the winter road wound along the banks of a normally rushing mountain river. But on this gray day the usually singing, shining stream was already locked in ice. Already chill winter weather had frozen the banks, frozen the quiet stretches, frozen its flow. It was grim and gaunt and oh so forbidding in its stern dark silence between the dark boulders along its edge.

Suddenly, as I mused over the melancholy mood of the sad stream, a sharp, clear incisive insight entered my awareness.

That is exactly what has happened to the very soul of this wanderer. His heart has been turned into ice. His spirit has shrunk to a mere trickle of joy by the adversity of his life. His whole being has become cold and frigid.

"*Oh Christ, have compassion on this, your wayward wanderer. He is so far from home, from family, from you!*" It was an inward cry of intercession for the lost.

Though I drove and searched and pleaded on his behalf most of that winter day I never did find the stray. I met a man who said he was sure this one with the hard heart had already moved on to a large coastal city more than 250 miles away. But there had been no forwarding address, no clue to pick up his tangled trail of fears and tears.

As I drove home in the gathering darkness of this winter day, a calm assurance swept through my soul that the effort had not been in vain. It never is if our motives are pure and our love for the lost is sincere. Our Father has His own gentle way of using our simple sacrifices to touch, enliven, and restore the wayward one.

I might not even see the day when this dear fellow is restored in love and warmth to the circle of God's family. I might well have passed over the "great divide" before the springtime of Christ's presence melts the chill ice in the stream of his soul. I may be long gone to glory before the warm wind of God's gracious Spirit flows and blows across the deep snows of this man's despair to turn his mourning into songs of joy. It may be weeks or months or even years until there is springtime in his soul again.

But spring does come! It will come to this mountain stream, bound in ice and set hard as stone. Spring will set the river to flowing in full force, singing again over its stones.

So, too, the wonder of our Father's forgiveness, the warmth of His compassion for the lost, the soft stirring of His gentle Spirit will draw this one to Himself.

The winter of the soul will be past.
The freshets of spring will flow in this spirit again.
There will be a new song in earth and sky.

Spotless Snow

For weeks a cruel arctic front held the hills in its grim and frigid grip. The skies were dull, leaden grey. The whole world longed for release from the deathlike deep freeze of frost and ice and wicked, cutting winds.

Sometimes it seems the adversities of evil, the darkness of despair, the frigid chill of false accusations can descend upon our spirits and lock them for a brief period in a deep freeze of discouragement.

That happened to me during the past few weeks of stern winter weather. So there was not only a deep chill outdoors, but also a sinister winter chill within my own soul. A severe poison pen letter had come from across the continent. It went on for pages and pages like a cutting north wind spewing out of the arctic waters. What made it doubly cruel was it came from a person to whom I had shown kindness and help in generous measure.

After quiet meditation, a letter of reply was written with patience and forbearance. Still it did not seem to sit right in my spirit. The envelope was left open, unsealed. The letter was read and re-read but not mailed. Was it my Father's will to reply in this way or not?

Then suddenly one afternoon the dark clouds parted. The

sun streamed through the overcast. All the world became a glistening wonderland under its spotless mantle of fresh fallen snow. I pulled on warm clothes and went out to hike in the hills. The chill of winter was broken by the glorious, intense sunshine now reflected off the spotless snow radiating across the whole region.

In a flash of intense inner illumination I was also suddenly set free from my spirit's deep freeze of despair. *Don't send the letter—Don't defend your actions; you have been reviled but do not reply—Christ was silent before his accusers.*

In a shining instant of inspiration I saw clearly my conduct; my character was covered by the spotless, snow-white righteousness of Christ. It was enough. All was well within. His life, His love, His light enfolded me.

I went home in joy. The letter went in the wastebasket.
In that simple, single action there was repose.
The winter doubts had been removed from my soul.
The right thing, the proper response had been carried out.
A calm serenity, Christ's peace, enfolded my spirit.
My entire being rested in His approval.
His presence was bright all about me, and in me.

Yes, the brilliance of the winter sun had dispelled the dark clouds and leaden overcast outside with shining snow.
And the imminent, inner brightness of the Son of God had dispersed the darkness shrouding my soul inside with His intense righteousness.
No wonder His Word declares boldly:
*"Though your sins be as scarlet
They shall be white as snow."*

This was not just poetic imagery spoken by the prophet of old.
It was much more than merely a metaphor.
It transcends the entrenched teachings of the ancients.
For me, an ordinary man, troubled in soul, tempted to

try to acquit myself, attempting to justify my actions in an angry world, this was wondrous redemption.

This was to know first hand in living reality the dynamic life-changing, soul-cleansing companionship of Christ. With His coming there came His peace. With His coming there came His power. With His coming there came His purity.

And there was quiet rest!

The Berry Bush

The scraggly little shrub had taken root close against the concrete foundation wall of the garage. Whether it had been planted there deliberately by the previous owners, or had merely sprung up from a stray seed dropped by a bird, I shall never know.

One thing was certain, the struggling little berry bush was trying to grow in a tough, tough spot. For one thing it was so tight to the wall, so far back under the eaves overhanging it, that it seldom received a drop of rain, except for what blew in against the building in gusty winds. Secondly, it was standing in full sun facing south where daytime temperatures often scorched it with searing heat and burning sun reflected from the hot walls. Thirdly, it was growing ever so slowly in a mixture of waste rubble and sandy gravel hauled in as fill around the foundation.

Despite its unpromising location and misshapen appearance, it bravely put out a scraggly spray of white, sweet-scented blossoms the first spring we were here. I waited patiently to see what sort of berries would follow. To my great delight by fall they had formed into a fistful of brilliant ornamental fruit deep, rich tangerine in color. At once I fell in love with the gallant little shrub. Even in the midst of adversity it would glow with beauty. If given proper care, it could enhance this barren spot so blasted by sun, wind, and burning temperatures.

I went to the hills and gathered cattle dung off the open range. This was hauled home in sacks to be scattered about the base of the bush. The following summer it put on some astonishing growth. It seemed the struggle to survive had been won. But was it?

The following winter was ferocious and frigid. Fierce arctic winds, plunging temperatures, and record breaking wind chills did their deadly work on plants, shrubs, and trees.

Nor did the handsome berry bush escape.

As spring spread its warmth across the world, the shining green foliage of the berry bush began to turn brown. Not all at once, but by degrees. Here a branch, there a branch. It was almost as if they had been scorched with a blow torch. If ever a bush looked "beaten," it was this little favorite of mine.

Day after day I went out to stand beside it, sometimes in anguish of heart, wondering what to do. It had suffered tremendous damage from the winter weather. Should I just tear it out by the roots? Or should it be given another chance? If so, it would demand drastic action!

I loved the lowly, beaten-down, bedraggled bush too much to tear it out. Despite all the discouragement, we would have another try to restore its life and redeem its loveliness. Would it respond?

Taking a sturdy, big pair of branch loppers in hand I went out to do the awful cutting that was required. It almost hurt my spirit to be so severe. But every weakened branch was pruned back, almost to ground level. There were piles and piles of brown branches, dead, dying, strewn around on the gravel ground. All that remained was a handful of short, stark stubs close to the soil that still bore a few brave leaves of tender green.

The question was, *Can it come back to full life?*

For weeks and weeks I watched, I waited, I wondered.

It was as though its very life trembled in the balance.

It was touch and go.

Yes or no?

Then as by a miracle, new buds began to form at the base of the old beheaded branches. Slowly, slowly, but surely, surely they began to fill out and form. I was filled too with fresh hope.

A few days later the first tinge of tender green foliage began to burst from the tired old branches. A sudden, startling surge of new life pushed out in new shoots with rapid growth.

All summer long I watched in wonder as I watered it with tender loving care.

By autumn it had matured into a magnificent big bush, almost as tall as myself, with sturdy branches extending out wider than my long, outstretched arms. It was pure pleasure to behold! It stood like a shining symbol of renewal adorning the garage wall. But was it tough enough, hardy enough, to handle another winter? Only time would tell.

Last spring the entire shrub, from the lowest limbs to the topmost twigs, burst into a glorious display of showy white blossoms. Their fragrance filled the air. Insects swarmed over the blooms in hordes. Bees, wasps, butterflies, and beetles hovered over the bush gathering the sweet nectar, pollinating every flower.

Never, ever, in a long lifetime of tending trees and shrubs had I witnessed such a fabulous set of fruit. Thousands upon thousands of berries took shape. Steadily they ripened from green, to yellow, to rich red color. In the sunrise and sunset this glorious bush appeared as if it were on fire, incandescent with an inner glow of burning light.

The birds were quick to find this fall banquet. The robins, the waxwings, the other fruit eaters came in their hundreds by day to feed on the bountiful feast. And so did the deer, the coons, and the coyotes by night. All of us, all of us—birds, animals, and a contented man—had much to cheer about. Why? Because a lowly little bush had been brought back from the very brink with tough but tender care.

In quiet moments outdoors beside the shrub, I have stood alone in silent awe, acutely aware that my Father, the great, good, gentle husbandman (gardener) has done the same for me. His loving care and deep concern for me called for endless patience, enduring perseverance, unusual skill to restore my soul and reclaim my spirit from destruction.

There had to be digging. There had to be dunging. There had to be drastic cutting and pruning and shaping. Yet all done in love and affection—constantly refreshed by the water of His life. Out of His refreshment has come fresh foliage, fresh flowers, fresh fruit to nourish all around.

Gentle Thaw

For weeks and weeks our mountain world was rigid with frigid temperatures far, far below freezing. The lakes, the mountain slopes, the trees, and the shrubs were frozen hard, stiff, and brittle. It was as if the earth itself was held hard, unmoveable, in a vice of ice. The grim grip of arctic air from the northern tundra had a still, chill command of the climate.

So beneath the stark whiteness of winter all of us hovered in our shelters. Men in their houses with thin, blue plumes of wood smoke rising from the chimneys. Animals huddled helplessly in the forest thickets struggled to survive. Birds, what few remained, fluttered feebly in the trees and snow-laden underbrush searching for sustenance to ward off the wicked winter weather.

Snow, ice, and biting winds were no longer merely an adornment of the season. They had become a cruel, crushing enemy that subdued the spirit and dismayed the heart. The long, long nights; the brief, bleak days of gray skies, gray clouds, and gray outlook weighed down the world. It was like living in a white, stark cemetery where nothing moved, no life could be seen, and all hope had been buried.

Then yesterday, beneath the soft impulse of a soft south wind, the whole region began to stir and change. It was as if, and it was in fact, the impact of the warm flowing air from the far reaches of the south Pacific had touched us.

At first there was a ferocious fall of new snow. The mois-
ture-laden air deposited a huge fallout of heavy flakes along its
moving front. In moments a heavy blanket of fresh whiteness
lay over all the earth.

But beneath its soft covering I was startled to hear the delicate "drip"—"drip"—"drip" of snow melt sounds dropping down
the drain pipes outside my office window. The muted notes were
like the first gentle notes of a great symphony. I was stirred.

I had not heard such music for months. . .not since the
last autumn showers dampened the soil and ran in tiny, tumbling notes off our red, roof tiles. Could it really be that suddenly, swiftly, silently a true thaw had settled into our ice
bound world?

In unbelief comingled with pure pleasure I pulled on heavy
winter boots, struggled into a smug wool jacket, clamped a warm
cap over my head, and went out to explore the scene. Sure enough,
the mellow, moist air flowing over my face was the warmest to
the senses that I had felt on my cheeks in weeks and weeks.

Then it began to rain. Yes, real rain. Gentle rain. Warm
rain. As if by a miracle, frozen needles on the trees, frozen
limbs, and frozen shrubs began to glow and glisten. They actually loosened up and grew pliable bending in the breeze, shed-
ding their snow, and sparkling green again.

I went to hike in the hills. The heavy cloud cover began to
break open under the impulse of the warm wind. Ragged gaps
were torn open in the overcast. In bursts of pure glory the sun
streamed through to fill the hill, the trail, and the snow beneath
my boots with laughing light. The sunshine sparkled with an almost blinding brightness on the snow now melting all around me.

For the first time in months I pulled off my wool mitts and
bared my imprisoned hands to the warm air. It was sheer joy to
open my jacket and let the south wind play around my face, my
neck, and my cheeks. What splendid release! What joyous refreshment! Fresh hope sprang up within. My spirit was set free.
I climbed the heights in glee with surging strength.

Fresh deer tracks crisscrossed the trail. They, too, were on
the move. In minutes, by treading softly, I came across a band
of five handsome specimens, three does and two fawns. They

had been foraging out in the open, drawn by the thaw. Now they relaxed in its warmth, relishing the winter sun that touched their hill. It was a moment of truth.

As I came down off the trail in the twilight, there came home to my heart with tremendous impact an acute awareness that this day outdoors was so similar to some of our inner intervals of spiritual struggle. The parallels are profound. The same principles pervade both realms—that of the physical world without and that of the spiritual realm within.

There simply are those spans of time in our walk with God that for one reason or another "winter weather" does descend upon the soul. It may be some adversity that locks us in its cruel grasp. Perhaps some illness or some persistent pain imprisons us for long periods. There can be deep disappointments that chill the spirit and constrict the soul. We may find our wills hardening against the hard knocks of life. We may even become resentful and stiff and sense imprisoned within the stark dark walls of our own self-pity. Our outlook can become bleak and bare as we stare out at a gray, gaunt world.

What we need in this "winter of the soul" is a gentle thaw. We need the irresistible impress of the warm wind of Christ's gracious Spirit to touch us again. We need the melting, mellow, transforming sense of His presence enfolding us.

> There is unalloyed awe and wonder in His coming to us!
> I know of no other such influence that is so welcome.
> The gentle wind of His grace and His care bring joy.

For it is out of the enormous depths of His compassion, like the south wind off the Pacific, that there flows to us His power. From the immensity of His own abundant life there comes to us the life-changing impact of His transforming love. He strangely warms our souls. He softly sets our spirits to singing a new song with a new sound. He silently but surely enlarges our horizons, widens our vision, inviting us to crawl out of our old confinement to walk with Him again in the high country.

The searching question is, "Will I respond to His clarion call, 'Just follow me. Come to me. I will give you respite and rest from the struggle of your soul'?"

The Old Snag

The rough, rugged giant Douglas fir stands alone in a steep, grassy glade on a remote mountain range. I go there from time to time to take long tramps alone in quiet company with God my Father. The great tree dominates the wild terrain. Its broad-sweeping, broken, battered branches frame the open alplands of the distant ranges across the lake below. This is the sort of scene of which artists dream and from which I as an author draw deep, enduring uplift of spirit.

Yesterday for the first time this year I stood again, alone in the presence of the old snag. Its whole world is buried beneath a thick quilt of incandescent white snow. More than ever its gnarled trunk stood strong, superb, and serene in its stark setting. Its tough, wind-tossed branches, battered by a thousand winter storms, still reached for the sky in defiance of all the snow that they bore so bravely.

In more than a century of adversity it still stood in noble grandeur and quiet beauty on its harsh ridge. In the utter stillness of the winter's silence I stood and mused upon its gentle majesty. Never before had it impressed me so forcibly with its strong towering might. Slipping my camera from its leather case, I composed a picture of the mountain monarch standing in great strength against a glistening, shining backdrop of northern mountain slopes.

It seemed such an appropriate action!
It was a salute of honor to a gnarled old veteran.
It was a token of gratitude for such grandeur.

For the first time in looking at the old snag closely I noticed a large, recently evacuated woodpecker hole near the top of its trunk. It spoke worlds without words. Disease and decay had set into the old heartwood. The passing years, long years, had ravaged its strength. One day soon it would crash in a storm.

But in the meantime, yes in the time still left to it, its presence still stirred my human spirit. Its tough old form still gave shelter to a family of woodpeckers. Its crop of cones nourished a whole new generation of squirrels. And in summer its massive boughs gave gentle shade to the deer or the steer that chose to rest beneath its branches.

In more ways than one the grand old snag was a benefit to all who shared its lonely upland realm. All of us who came within the compass of its company were richer for it. The old fire snag did just that to artist, author, bird, or beast. Each was richer for having spent some time here.

Standing there, deep in thought, amid a pristine scene of immaculate mid-winter purity, the wondrous Spirit of the Most High impressed upon my own inner spirit a profound parallel. There were no audible sounds in the acute solitude. But there was a momentous, moving, muted inner conviction of the utmost clarity.

"Phillip, you too, are an old snag.
Your years have been long. They have been strong.
You have spent much of your time in solitude, in silence."

And now, yes now, your years are quietly, inevitably coming to a close. You, like this noble old tree, are a small but significant part of the passing scene. Nothing on earth endures. Only God Himself remains forever unchanging.

But in His presence, under the impress of the wind of His Spirit, you too have withstood a thousand storms that shaped your life. Your gnarled roots have been grounded deep in the solid rock of Christ's character. Your life has been nourished by His Word, fresh every day, springing up within your soul.

Because of this you have brought inspiration and uplift to others. The outreach of your witness to the goodness of God has given shelter to those who drew near to you. Yes, even in old age you provided comfort to those who came. Nourishment to those who sought it.

"Phillip, you are an old snag, but, you did not live in vain!"

The Covey of Quail

The morning was quiet, passive, waiting for the low winter sun to break over the eastern ridges. There was that muted promise in the air that the day would be sharp with frost but yet mellowed with sunlight sparkling on the snow.

Softly I strolled along a sheltered stretch of a river bank where running rapids had shattered the ice. Splinters and slabs of the pale blue ice floated in the running water. Some piled up along the bank forming little bays and backwaters where ducks and geese could dabble in the shallows.

Upon my approach the wary birds took wing. Or if not, they quickly dived into the main current and were soon swept downstream. I followed at a distance, treading softly in the deep snow piled up around the shrubs, trees, and wild thickets of brambles that grew in abundance along the banks.

As I worked my way along the stream, I wondered to myself why it was I had not come across a single quail. Generally the wary birds gathered here in large numbers. But this day it seemed there was no sign of the wild ones. Why?

Casually I passed a rather large clump of wild roses that tumbled over the rocks in a tangle of thorny brambles. I thought I heard the muffled cry of a quail in the undergrowth. But it was an unsure sound, and since I saw no bird tracks in the snow, I felt sure it was but a trick of my imagination.

On and on I hiked along the river. Somehow the whole world seemed strangely silent. No birds. No quail. No cheerful calls ringing across the river. It was as if I had rambled through a dead and desperate realm destitute of life.

Disappointed, I turned around at last and started to retrace my steps. At least I did not have to break trail again. I could move more quickly now, placing my big boots in my own deep footprints in the snow. I moved ahead swiftly, using less caution because it seemed there were no more birds to be seen on this barren day.

My rapid movements and hasty passage must have startled a covey of quail sheltering in the rose thicket. Suddenly about a dozen birds burst out of the brush. I stopped in full stride to watch them sail across the stream with rapid wing beat. I took a few more steps to be met with another explosion of quail hurling themselves out of the undergrowth. Then another and another and another flight broke from the bushes like fighter aircraft launched in rapid succession off a remote hidden airstrip.

I stood there stunned. Never, ever, in all my years of outdoor rambles had I watched such an impressive gathering of quail in a single spot. A very conservative guess would be that over a hundred birds catapulted themselves into the air with a rush of wings that carried them across the river to land in a thicket of trees on the other side.

When the last bird had flown in an urgent effort to overtake its companions, a sudden, searing, searching realization swept over me. It came as unexpectedly as the appearance of the quail themselves.

Their behavior is just like so many believers!
    Their stealth, their silence, is like so many "secret" Christians.
        They congregate in their safe sanctuaries, away from view.
            They do not want to be discovered, much less disturbed.

They find comfort in each other's close company.
They hope they won't be heard at all.
They just want to be left to themselves.

And yet all the morning, here was a man, a lonely man, who would have loved to hear their happy cries of good cheer. His spirit would have soared with fresh hope of approaching spring if he had seen them strutting about bravely in their wintry world.

The drastic, sharp-edged, cutting drama cut me to the quick. Was I like these quiet quail that preferred to play it safe? Content to just cuddle up in the cozy complacency and comfort of the church?

Or was I bold enough to be different? Bold enough to send up a cry of good cheer for the forlorn ones who shared my weary, old world and waited to hear and see and share my life of hope in God?

The Sun's Silent Strength

The sun in all of its majestic splendor is the epicenter of our solar system. Because of its remarkable size and immeasurable weight it exerts an enormous gravitational pull upon every planet.

It is this stupendous, unseen, silent strength that draws each object in space towards itself.

But there is more, much more, than just size and scale to the sun. There is tremendous energy, light, and heat generated within this sphere of fire. It radiates across the gigantic spans of space to illuminate our earth home. It brings light out of darkness, life out of what would otherwise be death, warmth and renewal out of desolation.

We see this every spring day when the golden orb is lifted up (or is said to be lifted up) above the southern skyline. Our spirits soar in anticipation of the light, the warmth, and the new life it will draw from the darkness of the dark winter nights.

Because the sun is lifted up above the horizon of our lives, hope leaps anew within our souls. The sun draws us, all of us, to itself. It draws men and women, boys and girls, from the close confinement of their homes. It draws squirrels and small creatures from their winter nests to bask in its rays. It draws rivulets of running streams from snowbanks, frozen ice, and giant gla-

ciers. It draws blossoms from their buds, green shoots from the
soil. It draws sap up the trees, birds into glorious flight and
song. The sun draws us all into a whole new dimension of life
with itself.

This profound principle has suddenly pervaded my whole
being.
The Lord God Himself, Jesus the living Christ, is a sun.
He, the Sun of God, is also the Son of God: God very
God. When He too is lifted up, He draws all men
to Himself.

He draws us by His greatness and majesty.
He draws us by His gentle grace.
He draws us by the light of His own superb glory.

Christ never ever withdraws from drawing us. No more
than the sun in space ever suspends its unrelenting influence
upon the planet earth. Its attraction is unceasing. Its silent
strength stretches across the immensity of outer space to sustain
us in its sphere of power, to retain us enfolded surely in its
gentle warmth and life giving light.

Christ comes to us, comes to us, comes to us. He draws us,
draws us, draws us. His beautiful benevolent influence is everywhere at work in the world. His power, His love, His strength,
His compassion, His presence, and His peace are here drawing
us into a brand new dimension of life.

He brings springtime to the soul.
He can be the sun in our sky.
He can be my very life.
But I must want this to be so.
I must come out of my own confinement.
I must fling aside the old clinging clothes of
coldness.
I must dare to go out and walk in the light
of His presence and power and peace.

Surely, surely, if squirrels or buds or birds can respond to
the touch of the sun and turn to feel the caress of its warmth, so

can I respond to the touch of the Master on my life. He comes to me in tenderness, but He also comes to me in strength. And always His first words are, *"Be not afraid—Be of good cheer—It is I—I am here!"*

He is here to draw me to Himself.
He is here to warm my cold heart.
He is here to bring His own good cheer.
He is here to assure me of His care.
He is here, so all is well.
My part is simply, quietly, sincerely, to open my life to Him.
He does the rest.
He brings rest.

A Note from
the Nuthatches

I t had been a gloomy day. Low, leaden clouds hung heavy over the valley. Veils of co-mingled mist and rain and snow drifted over the drab landscape. A chill wind, raw and ragged, cut its way over the ice-crusted slopes and ice-locked lake.

But despite the darkness, I was determined to take a walk, to get alone with my Father, to give Him a chance to speak softly but surely to my spirit.

For within my soul—my mind—my emotions—my inner will there was gloom as well. It had been spawned by a lengthy article I had just read about Stephen Hawking. He is considered to be the most brilliant scientist to impact the 20th century. Many of his peers consider him a greater genius than even Einstein. His book, *A Brief History of Time*, has been an international best seller with sales exceeding any other book of its kind. He has had more honors, more accolades, more attention given to his theories on the origin of the universe than any other scholar of this century.

The terrible tragedy in all of this academic exaltation is that he declares flatly, bluntly, without any embarrassment that *"he does not believe there is a God who created the universe and guides His creation!*" Not that there is anything new about this stance in the scientific community. It is an ancient challenge, a relentless cry of rebellion, against the Most High. It goes on from generation to generation.

I, too, as a young man in the university, was exposed to all the nefarious teaching, false theories, and vicious attacks made against Christ by the so-called wise men—intellectuals. And their subtle deception came within an eyelash of fracturing my faith in my Father above. So I could understand to some extent the reasons for Hawking's academic arrogance. My own spirit had become haughty, proud, and lifted up to defy the Most High. It had taken years and years and years of patience, perseverance, and compassion for Christ to draw me to *Himself*.

But with Hawking there had been one amazing difference. Though a man crippled in body, deprived even of his speech, he had been loved and sustained by his wife, Jane, through all his adversity. She was a devout and earnest Christian, unashamed to declare openly that it was in fact her own quiet, unshakable faith in God which had strengthened her amidst all the adversity. She could not possibly endorse her husband's assertion that "*there is no God, who is the Creator*" when in truth it was Christ who had undergirded her.

From time to time, in tenderness, but also in truth she had to remind Stephen—"*remember, you are not God!*" Therein lay the titanic tragedy of this man, this genius, this giant thinker of our age. Eventually, of necessity, the two felt compelled to part paths. Their profound, private, personal convictions were irreconcilable. That too is the great cost of following Christ.

It was this whole theme which weighed upon my soul as I tramped along the chill, stark, dark lake edge now heaped high with piles of ice. It was not easy walking. Drifts of snow covered glass-smooth mounds of ice where a sudden slip could quickly end in broken bones.

I paused to rest and get my breath beneath a stunted, wind-blasted pine growing out of a broken rock ridge. As I stood there silent, still, I heard the faint, single note of a nuthatch above me in the boughs. I looked up to see, not just one solitary bird, but a whole flock of nuthatches. As soon as they realized they were discovered, they all spontaneously broke into a contented chatter, no longer secretive.

Swiftly, surely, happily they fluttered from branch to branch, up and down the rough bark, gathering a ready banquet for themselves. Here amid all the gloom were these cheerful creatures, with joyous abandon relishing their bounty from our Father's hands.

The splendid, sweet assurance swept into my spirit. *"Oh my Father, you care for nuthatches in mid-winter. You care for me. You are here!"* It was a note of pure praise that set me singing.

In an instant of time, the happy, light-spirited chatter of the nuthatches had set my own spirit alight with the ignition of renewed confidence in my Father's care for a world all awry. It was Christ Himself who had stated so clearly, so emphatically—

"Look at the birds (the nuthatches) in the air! They do not sow and reap and store in barns, yet your heavenly Father feeds them. You are worth more than the birds" (Matt. 6:26 NEB).

Yes, yes, yes!

We human beings with our minds, our imaginations, our ability to reason, our emotions, our wills, and our sensitive spirits needed nourishment beyond bread and water, beyond merely the physical food sufficient for birds. We needed desperately our Father's care for all of life—body, soul, and spirit. And in the ever darkening days of our decadent generation we are in dire need of supernatural light from above to break through the gloom of despair that engulfs our generation. Again only God Himself could ignite and rekindle my faith in Him by the simple, lucid, living example of my feathered friends.

Let the sophisticated scientists strut their stuff.
Let the profound professors parade their human knowledge. Let the "wise-ones" (*Homo Sapiens*) declare God dead.
Let our arrogant academics despise and reject Christ.
Let our generation scorn our Creator.

Despite the worst they can do, He will have the last word. He always does!

And for me, a solitary man on this drab, mid-winter day, it took only the single note from a nuthatch in a wind-blown pine to set my soul aflame with fierce faith in my Father's care. That simple bird call was a note straight from Him to me. In a flash of bright illumination, piercing the gloom, it dispelled the darkness and set my soul to singing.

Thank you, my Father, for your precious presence!

Winter Wood

There is a serene sensation of repose and good cheer when one walks into a home heated with a wood fire. A fine fragrance of wood smoke like a primitive perfume permeates the atmosphere. The crackle and chatter of wood fibers, pitch, and resins exploding into flames are reassuring sounds of warmth and comfort in the home. The multicolored flames of orange, red, amber, gold, and even blue and green are a solace to the spirit, a delight to the eye.

Best of all, the radiant heat which emanates from the red hot embers is a living, pulsing dynamic warmth. It invites the visitor to draw near, to stand beside it, hands outstretched, eager to receive its gentle benediction. It beckons one to draw up a chair, put up your feet, and bask in the pure pleasure of its company.

I have such a spot, a very precious place, where I love to relax with a good book in close company with a wood fire. An old-fashioned wood lamp-stand is at my side where a soft glow of light illuminates the pages. Just behind it stands a simple, elegant set of bookshelves holding a superb collection of noble works. Some of them have been read and re-read across the years, always relished and treasured.

Yet somehow, in some special way, each volume takes on

new life, new meaning, and new delight when read again in the gentle company of the fire. Let the winds of winter howl like hunting wolves at the windows. Let the frost coat the glass and freeze the ground hard as rock outside the door. Let the snow pile deep in menacing drifts around the house. Still within, because of winter wood, all is snug and safe and wonderfully secure.

The pungent, delicate aroma of wood smoke fills the air.
The happy crackle of burning wood cheers the room.
The superb warmth of the fire brings comfort and quiet contentment.

Why? Why is so much pleasure, so much peace, and so much profound assurance locked up in a few logs of wood? Just the other day as I cut, split, piled, and carried armloads of the rough fuel, I began to reflect quietly on this question.

There is something beyond the common joy of heading up into the hills in search of dead or downed trees that can be cut for firewood. There is an inner secret to wood that is far deeper than the pleasure of piling the logs in a truck and hauling them home down a mountain road as insurance against winter. There is a subtle dimension to burning wood, more meaningful than the beneficial exercise it provides or the basic heat it supplies.

That simple secret is the life, the energy, and the very light locked in its fibers. It is an amazing principle. For across the long, long years of the tree's steady growth there was transferred into its very fiber the life, the energy, and the light of a hundred summer seasons. The constant, steady, on-going exposure of the leaves, needles, branches, bark, and buds to the sun had transmitted its qualities to the tree. More than even that, the very energy of the sun was transmuted into the wood. . . yes, wood that when burned gave off the same light and heat and energy stored within its cells by the sun.

What the burning logs now gave off is exactly what they got from the source outside themselves. All the benefits a wood fire bestows have been drawn from the incandescent star in outer space which we call our "sun."

With piercing intensity the principle of energy transfer held me.

In profound awareness my spirit was stilled by the parallel.

If the expenditure of my little life (this little log if you will) is going to bring warmth, cheer, light, and contentment to others, it must be from a source other than myself. It must be from the *Sun*, (The Son of God), Christ Himself.

This only happens by constant, continuous, open exposure of my life to His. So by degrees, day upon day, His very being is imparted to me. I am indeed a tree of His design.

Nor will the light, the life, the lovely warmth of His character imparted to me ever be seen, felt, or known except I too be broken, bruised, and battered as He was and is. I cannot remain comfortably wrapped up like an uncut log or unsplit block of wood and expect to make an impact on others.

Wood takes a terrible beating in order to be burned beneficially!

The tree must be felled.
The branches are stripped and torn from the trunk.
The prostrate log is sawn asunder into short lengths.
Then blocks are split apart with terrific blows.
Smaller slabs are further shattered.
Some is slivered into thin kindling.
Then it is fit to be lit.
Now at length, it can share its strength.
This is the winter wood that does such great good.

So it was, my soul began to understand some of the inner secrets to our life with God. Some of the deep, dark questions became clear. Some of the mystery to His ways with us was dispelled as I split up a pile of winter wood.

No wonder there were times when I was cut to the ground.
Now I see why my hard heart, my tough inner will,
my "heart wood" needed to be shattered, broken,
split apart. . .why I was stripped of human support.
At last I grasped why only the laying open of my inner person with all its anguish could help others.

Some of us are slow, slow, to perceive the principles of the Most High. I am one of them!

But one more thing is sure. If we are going to be on fire for God, it is not all fun and games. There is bound to be some pain and flames. Only He Himself can provide the courage and strength to endure the ordeal.

As we do, others will be glad we were expendable. And Christ will gain honor in it all.

Wilderness Call

The high-pitched, trembling notes wavering on the winter wind carried across the ice-clad lake. They wafted through the timber where I tramped alone. But ever as of old, that wild, tremulous cry of the coyotes stirred my spirit. It was a wilderness call which, if properly understood, spoke clearly of more than a small timber wolf setting off on its evening hunt.

The coyote is perhaps the most astonishing mammal on the North American continent. He has extended his far flung range from the edge of the tundra in the north to the hot deserts of the Southwest. His haunting call is heard from coast to coast. Despite all of man's attempts to destroy him, his cunning wit and tenacious spirit have overcome adversity so he could adapt to the radical changes of his environment. . . even to man-made towns and sprawling cities.

His melancholy melodies are carried on the winds of change that sweep across our western world. They are a warning cry that change is everywhere. Most who hear the haunting sounds think only that it is a throwback to the wilds. No, no, the high, thin, tremulous call is a warning, an alarm that change is in the air; change is everywhere.

Only those of us closely acquainted with coyotes and all

things wild can clearly comprehend their call, can understand the music that they make, and can interpret the high-pitched cry that carries on the winter wind.

I stopped in mid-stride as I heard the stirring sound. In an instant I knew what it foretold. It spoke clearly of a sudden change in weather. For weeks we had not seen the sun. Heavy overcast, snow-laden clouds, and chill temperatures had held the earth in a grip of ice. The sophisticated satellite photographs and "wise" weather forecasters had predicted more weeks of the same.

But the coyotes knew better. We were in for a change. And I knew it was true.

My spirit leapt within me with fresh hope.
The next day would bring open skies.
A sincere smile and grin of glee crossed my face.
A change was coming.
The sun would be back.
I hurried home to share the news with Cheri.
And it did!

Ever since the coyotes called, warm sunshine has gently enfolded our northern mountains. The warmth has changed the landscape, laid bare rock, soil, shrubs, grass, and pools of melt-water. A strange but strong stirring of spring pervades the earth. And another profound, powerful impulse of pure pleasure stirs in my soul.

There is a hint of spring in the air.
Change is everywhere.
New life, new light, new love are on the wing.
I rejoice in anticipation.

In exactly the same way there are sweeping changes now under way in the wilderness of our modern world. There arises a plaintive, wavering cry from our culture of great pathos. Only a few of us have ears to hear what that wilderness call really means.

Christ Himself, our beloved Friend, tried so hard to alert us to what this cry from the wilds of a world gone wrong would really mean. Not just more of the same. Not ever deepening gloom and doom. Not the deepening darkness of human despair, the chill grip of human greed.

The call of the wilderness was a cry of coming change.

Just as the coyotes knew the sun was coming back, so the wild cry of our world awry is a sure sign our Sun, our Savior, our Son of the Most High is coming back.

He told us, He tells us, He assures us, "When these things happen, look up, cheer up, the dawn is about to break in great glory. All will change! SOON!!"

White-barked Birches

In our mountain region white-barked birches are not a native species. It is too hot and too dry, for these elegant trees to thrive here on their own. But people who love the tall, stately trees use them in their landscaping, tending them with great affection, gentle care, and abundant water.

Just along the little country road a few hundred yards from my home two of the stately trees stand tall beside the lane. I walk past them to and fro every time I go to fetch the mail or take a hike in the hills. The two soaring spires of shining white swaying gently in the breeze against a glorious blue sky have become like two special friends. Their striking beauty, their elegant strength, and their graceful form are an enduring inspiration.

I have often wondered about this. Yesterday in the sparkling sunshine the trees seemed even more arresting than usual. Seeing them still bare-limbed, their buds not yet open, each long, slender, lace-like bough stretching towards the sky in gentle arches, I realized what their regal presence meant.

They stood like the twin spires of a spiritual sanctuary stretching towards the heavens. They were a constant reminder to a common man on a common road that his focus could be fastened on things above, on the things of God, on things of eternal value. The graceful white-barked birches in their gentle glory had lifted my soul in quiet inspiration and exultation a hundred times.

Clean, white, shining, and serene they stand strong in the sun. They embody all that is upright, dignified, and beautiful to behold. Quite dramatically, yet without ostentation or shame they are pure poetry. They speak softly but sublimely of the one who designed their character—Christ Himself.

I hope, I hope—I hope heartily—something about my simple life, my character, my conduct, and my consecration impresses onlookers a bit like my friends, these two white-barked birches.

Wild Swans

The morning was misty. Haze hung over the hills. All the world, our mountain world, was wrapped in gossamer veils of thin delicate clouds. There were no currents of air moving through the valleys. Stillness was supreme. It was as if all nature was poised, pensively waiting for a distant, profound sound.

Then it came! At first it was barely audible, a mere melody of muted notes drifting down through the mist. I scanned the sky with searching eyes. But the overcast was too dense to detect the source of this airborne symphony.

There was a pause, an interlude of intense silence; then again the trumpet-like notes pierced the cloud cover. At once my emotions soared in rich response. A skein of wild trumpeter swans were coming through the clouds. What a thrill so early in the year!

Moments later their snow-white, shining forms emerged from the heavy overcast. In fluctuating formation, their great wings flashing resolutely, they flew strongly above the ice-locked lake. They had come down the broad valley from the open water of the great deep lake north of us. For the few, fleeting moments of their passing I simply stood awestruck in wonder and joy.

Awestruck to see such a large number of the noble birds in a region where they were on the verge of extinction. When the first settlers came to this valley, wild swans were an abundant species. But drainage channels, ranch fields, and human abuse of the wetlands had devastated the nesting areas of this sky species.

But now in wonder and co-mingled joy I watched this flight exploring the region again in search of suitable habitat. There was some to be found. For in recent years an enlarged refuge had been established for wildlife. And in this protection of that preserve this wild remnant of winged royalty could not only survive but actually thrive.

With unabashed pleasure and excitement I watched the wild swans work their way down the lake deliberately. The sight of their flight and the glad cries of their going lifted my spirit in pure exaltation. A moving, deep, up-welling stream of genuine gratitude surged up within my innermost being.

What sweet satisfaction!
What deep delight!
What ecstasy!

All, all, all of this came unexpected, unannounced, as a gift-wrapped package in shining white from my Father's hands. It adorned the day with brilliance and beauty. Wild swans would grace our skies despite the worst modern men could do. They had brought good news of hearty cheer.

In those trumpet sounds there came to me another clear bugle call of immense spiritual uplift. In a flash I saw again how faithful our Father is to preserve a remnant, be it wild birds or that small flock of those humble souls willing and ready to follow Him.

When our Master moved amongst us in human form, He spoke simply but emphatically of how only a handful would discover the entrance way to eternal life in His company. But He assured us of His provision of a path for us, a place for us, and a remarkable care of His design.

He is forever at work in this mist-shrouded world of ours. The clouds may cover the scene; we may not always be able to clearly discern His divine designs in the overcast. Still, the great, heart-lifting assurance which comes to us who listen for His voice and look for His appearing is the lovely awareness, *"He is always at work behind the scenes!"*

Such acute awareness is strength for the soul, serenity for the spirit, and deep contentment for the day.

Yes, yes! Whether it is wild swans on the wing or the wings of His Spirit in His Word, we are renewed and made whole.

Hope leaps anew within the heart!

Hazy Hills

The winding country road that runs from my home into the nearby town is only about eight miles long, but it is one of the most tranquil and delightful drives I know of anywhere. It is only two lanes wide, cut out of the steep cliffs and rock bluffs that reach into the shining waters of the lake. For most of its length the road runs at the very edge of the shoreline. There, for some miles, are no houses to obstruct the views, only an occasional clump of poplars or a few sturdy sumac shrubs. The poplars glow like gold in the fall, and the sumacs flame red against the blue sky reflected in the blue surface of the lake.

The twenty-minute drive in and out of town is most often an interlude of pure pleasure. The setting is superb with the distant hills and mountain ranges standing sentinel on the sky-line. Some days they are clear and sharp and very impressive. Yesterday they were not more than a mere smudge on the horizon.

I was coming home gently, deep in thought, somewhat saddened by the hospital visit just completed. The winding road and the melancholy mood of the hazy hills complemented each other. I had never seen the mountains around the lake and around my home appear so remote, so distant, or so unreal. It was as if they had been painted on a giant piece of off-white paper, in the faintest hues of blue, in the thinnest of water colors.

The sensation that swept over me was sobering. *They hardly seem to be the same dear mountains I know so well and love with such fervor!* At best they appeared as hazy hills, far away, foreign to me.

In the pathos of that powerful impression a parallel thought of profound impact overwhelmed my spirit. *That is exactly the same way in which so many people see God.* He seems so remote, so distant, so hazy, so unreal, more like some artist's impression painted faintly on the parchment of their lives.

That had been precisely the case with those I had just visited in the hospital. All their lives they had claimed to be Christians; for years and years they had been active in the affairs of their church; to all outward appearances their spiritual life was solid and in order.

But was it?

Was their trust in our Father's care for them?

Was Christ Himself the source of their strength in this crisis?

Was the gracious Spirit present to give His consolation? Obviously not. For as I entered the room, the anxiety, stress, and distress were everywhere, very real, compelling, and palpable. It was as if in this time of extremity God was very far away indeed, like the hazy hills along the lake, not much more than a faint smudge of hope on the horizon.

As the patient gripped my hand in his, he remarked softly, *"There is no one I would rather see in here today than you."* I could only smile gently in response. For in my heart of hearts I longed earnestly that he might see the Master beside his bed. He needed to understand clearly that Christ was in that room near and dear amid his distress.

We shared some hearty chuckles.

We recounted the gracious faithfulness of our Father.

We prayed together in child-like entreaty.

Still I came away wondering earnestly if the Most High was someone so remote, so far off, so unfamiliar that faith in Him was little more than a faint illusion. I hoped not!

As I drove home the last miles, I gazed at the hazy hills and was gripped by a second superb sensation. *Phillip, aren't you glad you have spent years in close company with these mountains? You have climbed their ridges, explored their meadows, and relished their grandeur. They are near, dear, and very much loved. You are their friend!*

And it is exactly the same with God your Father, Christ your Friend, His Holy Spirit your Counselor! No need to fear! Here all is well!

The issue that commanded my acute attention in full view of the hazy hills was not one that would just go away. I suppose it was in part because the same faint landscape dominated every window and glass door of our home. More than that, it persisted for several days.

It was made even more intense when an eminently intelligent, bright, and successful businessman came to see me. He too was in a critical crisis. He faced the grim spectre of utter financial ruin and the bleak bareness of bankruptcy. In the chaos and confusion the presence of God Himself was little more than a thin blue vision on the horizon of his life.

It is in these ordeals of dark distress that faith in our Father becomes like a thin, delicate veil, very tenuous, easily torn away in the trauma of trial. Then those who have never yet come to know Christ will in close communion ask openly, "Where has God gone?" In actual fact it is a cry of despair in which they express disappointment with God.

Some of us have learned across the years in the crucible of suffering that "things are not always as they appear." Just because mid-winter mist, arctic haze, and thin, overcast skies make the mountains seem miles and miles away, they have not moved an inch. They remain unchanged. They still stand strong, sublime, and supreme in our surroundings.

Those of us who know them first hand—who have in very truth tramped their trails, shared their upland splendor, responded to their call, and revelled in their lofty inspiration—

love them with a passion. And because of this intimate association we turn to them again and again for our renewal in time of trouble.

So it must be with God our Father. When Christ becomes our close, beloved Companion and when His gracious Spirit is our trusted guide, we turn in the trail to find their presence real. No wonder we hear that glad refrain, *"I will lift up mine eyes unto the hills from whence cometh my help. My help cometh from the Lord!"*

"Bones"

That was his name when first he came to live in our neighborhood. It was an appropriate title for a dog of unusual conformation. All my life I have loved dogs. Even the most amazing mongrels have attracted my attention.

But Bones was almost beyond belief.

He was still a youngster when the neighbors got him.

The first time he walked past our home I had to look twice to be sure what I saw was real.

Bones was bequeathed the large massive head of an aggressive Alsatian (German Shepherd). He had the erect, alert ears; the large, brown, intelligent eyes; the lovely black and gold markings of the face; and the massive jaws and great gleaming teeth of a formidable guard dog.

But behind this bold front there appeared to be almost no body at all. In fact, the rest of Bones belonged to a slim, sleek whippet. The two breeds combined in one made for an unusual creature for which I felt enormous compassion. He seemed so thin, so pinched in the middle, and so hungry that I decided to do what I could to help fill out his frame.

What Bones lacked in body build he more than made up for with his ferocious bark. Still, I was not to be put off by his angry demonstration every time I walked by his owner's house. One

day I stopped to chat with his owners and learned they had changed his name to Watchful. It was quite a mouthful, but it showed their respect for him. At least they had high hopes.

I inquired if I could do my bit for Bones—sorry, for Watchful—by bringing over sturdy beef bones and fragments of fat for the fellow. I was sure this hardy fare would help to fill out his frame and get him through the harsh winter!

There was nothing heroic about this arrangement. More than anything else it was a simple gesture of goodwill, a mere matter of pouring some of my time, thought, interest, and love into this dear dog.

A few weeks later I was high in the hills, in deep snow, watching a band of deer browsing some fir boughs. Suddenly in wild panic they bolted off up the steep slope—snow flying from their feet. Behind them came Bones, all on fire with his tongue hanging out.

We were both on mutual ground. This was not his home territory. So with a sharp whistle and ringing command I called him off the chase. To my surprise he turned at once and came swirling to me in the snow. We greeted each other briefly. He recognized the scent on my hands, the same that bundled up the bones and packages of meat and fat I dropped off at his house.

Then he was gone, back down the mountain.

Later on as I tramped home in the twilight, I met his master and mistress searching for him. They could scarcely believe Bones had been on such a wild adventure. Just then he showed up, panting heavily. All of us had a hearty reunion, and I was assured he would not be permitted to run deer again.

Our short time together gave me a chance to pet him affectionately and thus become well acquainted. Never again did Bones bark at me. Whenever we meet, he greets me with bounds of pure pleasure and a soft smile of delight.

Bit by bit Bones is maturing into a splendid dog. He is developing into a rather remarkable companion who is intelligent, alert, and eager to please. His mistress assures me he has become like one of the family, a pet, a friend, and a Watchful guardian of their home. For all of this I am so thrilled. It just shows what love and care can do even for a dog.

The other day Ursula opened the front door. There stood a parcel. Inside was a beautiful big jar packed tight with beautiful, golden, home-preserved apricots. With it was a note printed with meticulous care. It read:

To Uncle Phillip and Auntie Ursula.

> My folks like my idea of saying my thanks with fruit. I love the bones.
>
> *—From Watchful*

Such a lovely gesture!
   An exchange of beef bones for golden apricots!
     A stirring example of our Father bringing a beautiful bonus out of something as bare as old bones.

I reflected on the incident and saw clearly in that moment that some of the choicest miracles that come to fill the empty cups of our days occur when we empty ourselves into other lives. Even if it is into an ungainly dog, called Bones.

Too often we moderns are looking for something special, something sensational, or something spectacular to impress us as a miracle. Yet all the time Christ stands beside us waiting to turn the ordinary events of our ordinary little lives into modern miracles.

Yes—something as bare as beef bones and table scraps of fat turned into warm friendships, a dog's affection, and golden apricots.

It was like the first miracle our Master ever performed in public at the wedding banquet in Cana of Galilee. All He asked of those around him was to fill the empty jars with water. He would do the rest and turn it into the finest, vintage wine.

Our part in all this pageantry is really very simple, very straightforward, and very much close at hand. Whenever we see an empty life, an open opportunity to pour in our affection, our care, our thought, and our time, Christ will do the rest. In His gracious, wondrous ways He can turn water into wine, hard hearts to warm hearts, and a dog called Bones into a guardian named Watchful.

But we must fill life to the brim. No half measures.

Singing Stream

There is a beautiful, surging stream running freely through the wild mountains west of us. It tumbles and cascades through rough terrain where high ridges reach for the sky. Its very source is the lofty mountain range of *"The Cathedrals"* where snowfields suckle its mountain springs.

This whole region is still, pristine wilderness where virgin timber cloaks the lower slopes, rugged as they are, and grass meadows lie open to the sun above timberline. Wildlife abounds in this realm—bears, deer, mountain sheep, mountain goats, cougars, coyotes, as well as lesser furbearers.

But the stirring, supreme center of this superb country is the singing stream that surges down the deep valleys over its rocky course. Gigantic boulders of all shapes, interspersed with innumerable small stones and scattered sand bars make up this stream's course. The ice-cold water, clear as the finest crystal, cascades around, over, and under all the obstructions, singing as it goes.

It is the very song of this stream which rises and falls, rises and falls in a never ending melody that is a balm to anyone who walks beside the cascade. It is the supreme music of this wilderness area, more powerful than the surge of wind in the timber or the call of the coyotes on the hills.

This music of the running water has an eternal quality to it. In its enduring loveliness there lies a gentle healing for those of us who come here for solitude and respite from the clamorous world outside.

Along the stream banks there is a profusion of water-loving trees and shrubs. Giant poplars with tough bark, elegant groves of black birches, red osier dogwood, and wild willows decorate the stream bed. They also provide an abundance of shelter and shade for birds, small mammals, and those of us who wander into the wilds.

Every year, without fail, both in the very early spring and late fall, I make precious pilgrimages to this place of peace. Two days ago the dawn broke clear and cold and compelling. The first rays of the sun to touch the high peaks burnished them in bronze and gold. In a matter of hours I was dressed in heavy winter clothes, had crossed the intervening ridges, and was tramping through the ice-crusted snow lying deep along my singing stream.

It was as if I had tramped back into a time when no man's tracks ever touched this wilderness. All morning I never saw another boot mark. There was not a single sound of human activity anywhere to penetrate the pristine solitude. Only the song of the stream pervaded this unspoiled bit of paradise.

Why did I come so far for such quiet moments?
Why take the trouble to tramp sturdily through the deep drifts?
Why endure hours of ice and frost and stinging cold?
Because of the singing stream!
Because of this intense solitude!
Because of the special inspiration of this setting that comes to my soul!

It seemed the stream and its surroundings all draped in gently sculptured snow had never seemed more lovely. As the morning sunlight reached down into the deep cut canyons, its illumination intensified the splendor of the setting. Every tree trunk, every rock along the watercourse, every stretch of tumbling rapids, and every snow pile shimmered with sunshine.

It was a scene of utter serenity far superior to any piece of artistry executed by a human master. This was a sublime masterpiece of divine design. It was of such gigantic proportions that it was possible to actually enter into its precincts as one would walk reverently into an ornate cathedral and stand awe struck in its stirring sanctuary.

Be still and know, yes know, I am God.
And in this stillness, Oh my Father, speak to me.

It has never been my claim to have heard the sombrous sounds of God's voice in audible tones. Some have done so. But there is a dimension of "hearing" the divine overtures of the Most High that far transcends the mere audition of sound. It is that supernatural awareness within the soul that stirs the spirit, and suddenly one is actually conscious that truth, inspiration, and inner illumination from Christ have come clearly and convincingly.

In a word, one *knows*! He has spoken!
In a sentence, His Spirit bears witness with my spirit inwardly.
In an instant, acute awareness of His presence prevails.

On this moving morning I knew assuredly my life had been touched, quickened, and ignited by the very life of the living Christ. And with that remarkable interaction came intense illumination—bright, sharp, scintillating as the snow-girt stream singing in this wilderness.

The parable was as pure as the whiteness all around me, as potent as the melody of the flowing water, and as profound as the pristine scene.

The impressions came in swift, sweeping, stimulating succession.

Phillip, my son,

> This stream is the very life of this wilderness.
>
> Likewise I am the stream of life in your weary world.
>
> The water of this mountain torrent refreshes
> and renews every creature that comes to it.
>
> So, too, invite everyone who is weary and
> burdened to come to Me for rest and restoration.
>
> The mountain melodies that rise above these
> running rivulets are pure sounds of healing.
>
> It is the same with Me—My music from eternity
> is pure, unpolluted—the glorious sound, "I love you."
>
> In company with this stream there is inspiration,
> peace, and inner calm.
>
> Those who share My supernatural life, also share
> the wonder of My sweet serenity and quiet strength.
>
> My beloved son—Walk with Me—All is well!"

Ice Thunder

I stood on a rocky promontory looking out over the frozen lake. Its surface was a dull gray expanse. On this afternoon, the ice, now nearly a foot thick, had the distinct appearance of old pewter, drab and tarnished.

But there was something powerful and provocative at work in the ice. A distant rumble, like the dull thunder of distant drums, would reverberate at one end of the lake, then come tumbling down its length in a growing crescendo. The sound muted by the ice itself would roar past my lookout point to fade away at the far end. Then just as unexpectedly, another surge of ominous sound would thunder from the ice and rumble across the valley like heavy artillery in battle.

Gigantic pressures and counter pressures were in play far beneath the surface of the sheet of ice. Gigantic fractures and gaping cracks would later betray where the breakup began. But the titanic thunder spoke now of the gigantic collapse soon to come. Unseen forces would fracture the gaunt and austere appearance of the icelocked lake. And down the future its face would shine again with the sparkle of sun on waves.

In that assurance a clear perception of our contemporary society and its dark, drab outlook engulfed my conscience. Like the lake, it has been caught in the icy grip of so much cynicism.

The culture of our times despises and sneers at that which is noble, honorable, and decent. Men's motives are so often sinister, selfish, and sordid. Warm hearts and shining smiles are becoming locked in lasciviousness. The shadow of human cruelty cloaks the earth.

There rumbles and thunders from the depths of our despair the ominous cry of children abused, the poor in perplexity, and the lost seeking solace. The distant drumbeat reverberates beneath the surface of our crass and crude civilization.

It speaks profoundly of the pain and pathos of our people.

But it forecasts also the soon coming of explosive changes. Christ will soon return—just as spring will soon be back to break up the ice.

The Tumble

W alking. Hiking. Climbing. All have been a joyous and important part of my life. Few indeed are the days that I have not pulled on a comfortable pair of walking shoes and headed outdoors for a brisk ramble. This chance to fill one's lungs with fresh air, to stretch the muscles, to exercise the heart, to revel in the wind off the hills, to rejoice in the sunshine, and to widen one's horizons is a precious part of living as a free and fit man.

These quiet interludes, especially if one is alone, are gentle times in which to think long thoughts. They are times to pray for others. They are quiet moments of close communion with Christ, of intimate interaction with my Father above, of inner peaceful promptings from His gracious Spirit, my guide.

Yesterday, though overcast and still a bit snowy from the storm the night before, was a challenging day for a brisk ramble. There was a bite to the wind, but not so chill that I was unwilling to go. I bundled up warmly with two wool sweaters, a heavy wool jacket, wool mitts, a wool cap, and heavy, double knit wool trousers that had taken me through scores of storms.

My step was jaunty, strong and eager. It surprised me how energetic I felt despite the rather adverse day. Swiftly,

smoothly I swung down the trail, cut across the open ice of
the lake, then headed up through the rock-ribbed hills.

To my pleasant surprise most of the winter's snow was
gone. Even in the sheltered spots on the north slopes and in
the lee of the trees the ground was bare and open. It invited
me to step out even more vigorously. Already I could sense
that spring was not far off. Then in a few short weeks the wild
flowers would be gracing these hills, their fragrant, brilliant
blooms adorning this wild and rugged terrain.

Suddenly, unexpectedly, in an instant, without warning,
my powerful right foot slithered away beneath my weight. I
could feel it sliding—sliding—sliding dangerously. All control
was gone, though I struggled vainly to right my weight with
the other leg. In a split second my balance was lost, and I was
tumbling down the steep slope.

Being rather agile and quick-witted I threw my weight up
the slope. It was fortunate I did, for I missed the rocks around
me. Instead, all humped up, I slithered down the trail in a pile,
stained with the soft black soil just starting to thaw. It was
smeared over my mitts, over my beloved warm jacket, over my
trousers, and over my boots.

Quietly I lay there for a few moments assessing the odd
twinges of pain that shot through my knee, my hand, and my
back. Nothing was broken, so I was glad. A few joints had been
stressed, but I was intact. A surge of gratitude rose within me.
Slowly I untangled my twisted limbs and got to my feet gingerly
and humbly. It astonished me to see how far I had slid down the
slope. The trail looked so safe, so sure, so secure. Then I discovered the danger. A slick of smooth ice had lain below the
melting surface of the earth. It was an unseen trap. And in an
instant it had brought me crashing down in a terrible tumble.

As I trudged home with much greater care, the thought
swept through my mind, *The tumble can come in a flash—without warning—and it is oh, so humbling.*

Life itself is a lot like that. So often we are rather cocky,
self-assured, strong in our own strength until—until—until
suddenly one day all unexpectedly we are flat on our face—
down on the ground—messed up with mud.

"Oh Father give me the gentle grace to walk hand in hand
with you.
Oh Christ, my Friend, keep my feet from falling by
your power.
Oh gracious Spirit, guide me ever in paths of
righteousness!"

First Redwings

A short distance from my home on the hill, about a mile as the ospreys fly, there is a small marsh. It is only about two acres in area. It lies quietly, tucked in close against high clay cliffs, ringed with brown and golden-stalked bulrushes. Here the mallards love to come and nest. Here the ospreys love to fish in the still waters. Here the redwing blackbirds love to sing in the spring.

But spring has been slow to come this year. Already it is long past the time when the golden buttercups burst from the brown earth on the south slopes. The hills are still cold and drab and dense. The whole world is waiting for winter to leave. The countryside seems spent with the severity of so much ice and snow.

But there is hope in the air.

Three days ago I passed the gentle marsh, so brown, so brittle, and so beaten back by winter winds. And there, there, clinging bravely to a cattail stalk was a solitary, brave, bold, redwing blackbird. His jet black plumage shone bright with iridescent intensity. His scarlet shoulders trembled with their glorious red epaulettes as handsome as any army general's full-dress uniform.

He was the first redwing from the far-flung marshes of the south, the first brave bird to cross the mountain passes of the west in northern flight to find his favorite marsh beside us. He was the first to fling his wild notes into the wind and declare to all the world, "Spring is here, even if you can't see it!"

In that sudden glimpse of the "little general," so utterly fearless and unafraid, my heart leaped up with joyous hope. Yes, spring was back! The birds were back! The sun was back! Even if all around seemed so stark and dark.

And the profound conviction caught up in my inner spirit. So it is, too, with our weary old world and its drab days. Christ is here. His Spirit moves amongst us. There is hope in the air. Our Father's faithfulness never falters. Life springs anew in my soul. He is here!

But a much more profound question, searching, searing, shot through my spirit as I glimpsed the gallant redwing alone in his dreary, drab surroundings. Did my presence, my life, or my coming bring similar uplift into my seared and sad society?

Was or is there something arresting, startling, or reassuring about my "just being here" that awakens onlookers to realize spring is here—to inject an element of good cheer into a social landscape of drabness and despair? Increasingly our culture is like a cold and cruel terrain, gripped by the grim vices of a realm gone wrong. Amid this ominous outlook, with so little hope, is there a sudden sparkle of spring because one of God's children is bold enough to be His redwing?

To be a speck of inspiration? To be a tiny bundle of brave life that proclaims the eternal faithfulness of our Father?

> Spring after spring the redwing blackbirds are back.
> Year after year more and more of their marshes are destroyed.
> Time after time they find new territory to nest in with courage.
> They simply will not give up or give in to a changing world.
> Despite the worst men do they just keep on singing?
> Amid all the chaos and confusion of civilization they bring in swift flight a flash of uplift, a note of hope, and courage to carry on.

The same should be true of us who follow Christ. . . who claim our confidence is in Him. . . who are not ashamed to own His name. . . who joyously share His abundant life.

When others see us, meet us, or watch us, our great good-will and joyous thrill at living exuberantly in Christ's care should be a contagion. Just being here, just showing up, and just fling-ing up our glad notes of gratitude to God for His goodness should bring assurance of springtime in the soul. Then others will be glad too that we are here!

> Yes a redwing in the marsh moved me mightily.
> And a joyous, jubilant child of the Most High can move
> others mightily no matter how dreary
> the scene may seem today.

March Storms

M arch is the month of storms in this mountain valley. It is the time when grim, gusting winds roar through the hills. The gales blow through the trees, bending their branches, shredding off the old clinging needles and bits of bark.

But the same storms sweep low across the open spaces blasting away all the dead and dying plants scattered across the open slopes. Stands of knapweed, wild mustard, tumbleweed, lambsquarters, milkweed, and a score of other species are torn from the soil, broken off at the roots, to be hurled across the landscape in the sweep of the wind.

It all seems to be a scene of wild confusion.

It is not!

It is seed planting time. The spring season of seed scattering . . . the powerful push for perpetuation of the species.

Year after year, century after century, millennium after millennium, wild plants, shrubs, trees, and grasses of a thousand diverse kinds have been perpetuated upon the planet by the seed dispersal of March storms.

The precious, tiny, dynamic germs of life enclosed in their

seed scales and assorted capsules or pods burst open in the
gales, fly far on the wind, then fall to the ground. Some seed
stalks are blown for miles. Wherever they go, they leave behind
a legacy of new life. This is how the landscape is adorned in
such diversity of greens. It is the secret to the delightful decora-
tion of the wild meadows with wild flowers. Actually this is one
of the ways in which our Father plants His untamed gardens all
across the globe.

As I watched the bundles of broken-off plants caught up in
the powerful wind gusts, hurtling over the hillsides, then lodging
beside some rock outcrops or shrubby copse, the wind of the
Spirit of God Himself drew near. In a split second, in the flash of
an instant, a tremendous truth awakened my inner spirit.

Our Father uses exactly the same process, the same principle, the same procedure to scatter the seed of His own life
across the landscape of our social world. Sad to say, many of us,
and I have been one of them, are too slow of spirit, too dull of
perception, to grasp His ways.

We often wonder why He chooses to pull us up by the
roots, so to speak, to send us off to some new spot not of our
choosing. At the time it seems a stormy, stressful ordeal. We
ask ourselves why does Christ choose to suddenly break us out
of our cozy old complacency and carry us willy nilly into a
strange new setting? We may even resent the rushing wind of
His Spirit who suddenly unsettles all the familiar events of life
and hurls us into new encounters across the community, across
the country, or even across the continent.

So often we are so preoccupied with our own security, our
own comfort, our own well-being that we are blind to His great
purposes for us. He really is not half as interested in my selfish
security, as He is in having me sent out to scatter the eternal
seed of His life in some bare spot. The way He put it when He
was here in human guise was this, *"As the Father has sent me into
the world, so send I you!"*

Just as in the realm of plants and shrubs and grasses, so
also in the realm of our spirits it takes some storms to get the
job done. Unfortunately, most of us try to take shelter from the
gusting gales of life. We do our utmost to avoid the crunching

winds that sweep into our experiences. Somehow we are very sure they are intended to destroy us.

In a sense that is so. *A seed left to itself never increases.*

For our Father does have His way in the whirlwind and the storm. The clouds of March are the sure sign of His approaching presence. The winds of adversity are also the winds of His design for seed scattering. Wherever we are taken, wherever we are blown, it is His purpose to plant there some of His own lovely life anew.

Am I willing to be battered, broken, blown about, to bring His on-going life to others?

Waiting Out the Weather

This was the morning we had planned to leave. All winter long, for four full months, we had hoped to get away. But again and again and again other calls to serve God's people had come just at the time a trip was arranged. So the plans were set aside and absolute priority was given to the tasks Christ called me to carry out with care.

Finally it seemed certain the way was clear to leave today. But just before retiring, the weather forecast called for an unusual late winter storm of co-mingled snow and freezing rain. The latter is the most hazardous peril on winding mountain roads. So again we decided to wait and see what the morning would bring.

At dawn I went outside to place our bags of trash where the waste truck would pick them up from off the curb. Just as I did so my foot shot from under me on a patch of black ice—unseen to the eye but dangerous in the extreme. It was the stern warning I needed. Again, no travel today. We would just have to wait out the weather.

Quietly I went down to my office. "Oh Father, you must have some reason, a special reason, for yet another delay! Just help me to accept it with goodwill."

He did!

For in my morning meditation He imparted to me a stirring new insight into trusting Him in utter simplicity.

Living a life of faith in God means never knowing where you are being led. But it does mean loving—knowing—trusting the One who is leading!

Therein lies strength, serenity, and surety of soul.

There was a transcendent sense of Christ's presence within. What if fresh snow blanketed the ice bound lake! What if black ice sheathed the roads! What if dark clouds hung low in the valley!

We would just calmly wait out the weather.

There was a divine design to this dull day.

What artistic touch of splendor would the master artist inscribe on the hours of this interlude?

We did not have to wait long.

The phone rang, and with its sound came the pressing call of a dear lady whom God is calling into His service. She was eager for direction, willing to consider flinging herself fully into any work Christ might have for her.

Such are the wondrous ways of our Father in not only leading us gently in the paths of righteousness, but also opening exciting new doors of adventure to others. Freely, openly, without fear, I could urge this dear person to put her entire confidence in Christ for the work to which He called her.

Joyously I encouraged her to trust Him for everything.

Trust Him for the precise place she should go.

Trust Him for the exact work she should do.

Trust Him for the chance to touch others profoundly.

Trust Him to bring the lost ones to Himself.

Trust Him to provide her care and support.

Trust Him to fill her life to overflowing.

Trust Him as her dearest friend.

When I hung up the phone, I turned to Ursula quietly and remarked softly, "That is why we had to wait out the weather!"

There was nothing startling or sensational about this incident. Still it was that sublime touch of our Father's fine design upon the canvas of this dull day. Suddenly there was a bright silver edge to the clouds. And out of such sparse surroundings there shone a soft glow of contentment more sublime than the shining of the sun itself.

It took only one slippery step on a sheet of black ice to warn me of the peril on the roads. But that same single step was also enough to keep me in the place of God's appointment for today.

Truly the walk of faith with God is literally *One step at a time.*

Renewal

According to the calendar spring is here. But outdoors in the harsh world of mountains, lakes, forests, and upland range there are few signs of any seasonal change. The lakes still lie locked in grim, gray ice. The chill arctic winds funnel down the mountain valleys from the far north. The foothills stand stark, their gaunt ridges bare and brown with no apparent promise of spring.

But yesterday all that changed.
I came home from a brisk hike in the biting wind.
Just as I scrambled up a steep slope immediately below our home, I was stopped in my tracks.

Pressed close to the soil, each no more than one inch high, glowed four tiny *buttercups*, growing in the shelter of the sage.

It seemed so impossible!
New life, new blooms, new leaves bursting from the earth.
In spite of every adversity here was astonishing renewal.
This was akin to resurrection from death and despair.
Here was hope!
I was in awe.

I rushed into the house to share the good news with Ursula. That is what our Father's renewal does for us.

A few hours later I was reading the annual reports of one of the Bible societies that we support very vigorously. Again to my unbounded delight another note of renewal, of inspiration, sprang from the printed pages.

In Denmark, a country which for roughly 50 years has rejected and ignored God's Word, there has suddenly sprung to life an enormous national interest in the Bible. So much so that booksellers unanimously pronounce the new *Bible* edition, *"This year's absolute front-runner. It will be under every Christmas tree."*

Talk about new life springing up out of a barren soil. This is it! Speak of spiritual renewal in the stark setting of a society far from the truth. Our Father has His glorious ways of bringing us *His hope, His renewal, His resurrection!* . . . In the most unexpected places.

Deer—Distress or Delight?

I n dismay I looked down at the only flower bed which has been planted in a sun-burned spot by the garage. The site is too hot, too blasted by the desert winds, and too tough to support most plants through our scorching summers. But it is the warmest place for spring flowers like tulips, hyacinths and daffodils. It had been ravaged!

Last fall in co-mingled hope, faith, and love for flowers I decided to try to get a flash of color from this bit of barren soil. I went to the hills and gathered up a load of cattle dung which I spread carefully over the rocky soil. The gleaming brown bulbs sheathed tightly in their shining husks were buried gently in the soil. Then a deep mulch of litter was laid over top to protect them against winter weather.

The green shoots of their first leaves had burst from the flower bed with exuberant energy. The buds soon began to swell and form with rich promise of glorious blooms. Then I went out at dawn the other day and saw the damage. My heart-beat almost hesitated a moment. I could hardly believe the scrambled deer tracks that churned up the soil leaving it looking like a cattle corral.

Not one, but several, deer had discovered the flower bed. And for them this was a banquet of fresh greenery, craved so

much after a long harsh winter. The leaves, the buds, the new
tender shoots were cut off at ground level. And some of those not
eaten had been trampled and torn by the sharp-edged hooves of
the invaders.

I have always, always, loved and admired wild animals. But
in this moment of distress I really was surprised at the sudden
uprush of antagonism that swept through me. The harsh thought
flashed through my mind, *These deer have thousands and thousands
of acres to feed on all across these wild hills. Why in the world must
they pick on my tiny flower patch?*

My angry animosity startled me.

In the stillness of the moment a sense of shame flowed
over me.

My hard, tough assessment of the damage was dead
wrong.

A second, searing, searching impulse shot through
my spirit.

Deer—distress or delight? Which was it to be? The profound, penetrating question burned its way into my innermost
being. I stood there in two minds, shuffling my boots in the
sun-warmed soil, plowed up by dozens of deer tracks. What was
it to be—distress or delight—over this apparently adverse turn
of events.

Gently, persistently, other questions came clearly.

"How many people live where deer and eagles and
coyotes and quail and coons are their next-door neighbors?"

"How many homeowners live in an area so peaceful, so
quiet, so serene those other creatures of hoof, wing, or paw
enjoy it? How great is the special joy, the rare pleasure, the
thrilling uplift that these wild ones bring with them!"

"Why then your animosity?"

"Why your anger?"

"Why, why?"

In contrition I hung my head.

The choice was mine as a man—*distress or delight?*

I was determined to take delight in the deer.

At dawn the next morning I looked up from my desk to see three magnificent mule deer just below our house. They moved across the grassy bench with noble dignity and proud carriage. I was thrilled through and through.

Again the following dawn they were on the hillside on the other slope above the house. Excitedly I called Cheri (my wife's pet name) to come and share the moment with me. Her eyes lit up like lamps and a radiant smile glowed across her face. Both of us gasped, "Aren't they beautiful!"

Yes, more magnificent than tulips or hyacinths.

In life the choice is always there if we will look for it.

Deer—distress or delight?

Planting Peas

T he forecast for the day's weather was rain and snow. But by breakfast golden sunshine streamed into our dining nook and all the outdoors pulsed with pure light.

It was a perfect morning to plant peas.

The seed had been soaked all night.

So the peas were plump and round, ready for the ground.

With painstaking care I prepared the smooth trenches where the seed would be sown in love and calm assurance. The soil was dark with humus, soft to the touch, and fragrant with the delicate aroma of fresh turned earth.

In fact there had never, ever been a garden in that particular spot before. It was a steep slope where only grass and wild weeds grew before. Now it was to be a garden.

I was actually working with a bit of virgin soil. Just the thought was a challenge of good cheer. This ground was rich and friable, nourished with the decayed grass and leaves from nearby trees. There was a sweet solace in feeling its rich texture beneath my finger tips. It would become a suitable seed bed for the peas. There would be a bountiful crop in this bit of soil to nourish us well in the months to come.

Planting peas was not just a profound pleasure.
Planting peas was the step to deep satisfaction of soul.
Planting peas, done in calm confidence, would give a
crop.

Softly, surely, with a contented melody within, I covered
the seed with special care. I did not wish to bruise or damage a
single pea, each so plump and turgid, ready and eager to burst
into new plant growth.

There is always a bit of mystery, a gentle miracle in planting any seed. Our Master put it in these plain words.

"*Unless a grain of wheat (or any seed) falls into the earth and
dies, it remains by itself alone, but if it dies (gives up its life), it bears
much fruit*" (John 12:24).

So it is too for any person prepared to give up their life for
others.

When the planting was done, I stood up tall and straight,
stretching my back to the unfolding warmth of the sun. Its rays
would soon warm the fresh turned soil. And under the quiet
cares of April showers a glowing crop of peas would soon push
up from this bit of barren ground.

Little did I even dream that before this day was done there
would come a couple of chances to plant a bit of my own life in
the soft soil of some other souls. I had just put away the garden
tools, washed my soiled hands, and sat down for a short rest
when there was a knock at the door. A young man accompanied
by a dear little girl had come distributing Jehovah's Witness
literature. I urged Ursula to invite them in. Quietly but earnestly I was glad to share with them the joyous good news of
Christ's wondrous love and mercy to us. They listened eagerly.
The interlude was as satisfying as planting peas had been. We
were caught up together in a joyous discussion of our Saviour's
deep desire to draw us to Himself, to deliver us from death, and
to share His very life with us. Ursula served them a sparkling
cool drink of apple juice, along with cookies. They left us glad
eyed, all smiles, promising to come back.

The day went on and supper was just ready to be served. A
car pulled into the drive. There were four people, two old friends,

along with a young couple from across the mountains. Supper was set aside. They were welcomed in and also served refreshments of fresh home-baked bread and sweet apple juice.

The young man and woman were also searching, prepared souls to know more of Christ. Happily, eagerly, we let the miracle seed of our Father's grace and compassion fall into the friable soil of their souls. It was sown in good cheer, in laughter, in love, and in formidable faith. There would be a harvest here as well!

This process was as sure as planting peas. All in one day!

Balm of Gilead

I t was one of those busy, busy days. Go here, go there, go anywhere, try to be everywhere! Meet this appointment, meet that demand, yes, and perhaps not meet the Master in calmness and quietness.

Suddenly, speeding down the road, an acute, compelling, arresting inner awareness of His presence pervaded my spirit. *Pull off at the next turn. Slip down to the sand spit in the lake. Take time to be still!*

I was more than thirty miles from home. There was a full, full day planned. There had never, ever, since dawn been a single thought of taking time for a gentle stroll. But, yes, I would obey.

To my surprise, as I walked down to the spit, there was scarcely another soul around. It seemed strange on such a stirring spring morning. The whole world was pulsing, vibrant, and energized with new life. Magnificent cumulus clouds climbed into the blue April sky above the mountains. Their glorious reflections adorned the lake in majestic beauty.

I stood, silent, pensive, waiting, and awestruck by the scene.

"Oh, my Father, thank you for such glory, such grandeur!" I inhaled deeply, again and again and again. Peace, His peace, and His presence enfolded me. The rush, the hurry, and the tension of the day ebbed away softly. All was still within.

A flicker flew out of a knothole in an old tough tree, proclaiming loudly this is where it would nest this year. A cool breeze began to riffle the glasslike surface of the lake. To keep warm I decided to walk briskly along the tree-edged margin of the spit.

In a matter of moments a potent perfume, unmistakeable in its pungency enfolded me. No other fragrance in all the world has ever stimulated my senses more in the spring. It is the one aroma of the wild woods that proclaims in great power, "The sun is here! Spring is here! I the noble, sturdy poplar of the north am here: The gallant balm of Gilead."

I stopped still in my stride. The branches above me were laden with the catkins of bursting buds. The sticky, sweet scales littered the sand. Their brown and green textures formed a lovely mosaic on the forest floor.

Balm of Gilead . . . What a precious tree! So much beloved by all wild creatures. Its perfume in the spring. Its green and whispering leaves for shade in the summer. Its cool groves where fawns find shelter and grouse chicks grow safely. Its gorgeous, golden banners that flutter so bravely in the fall. Its soft, tender, nourishing bark that beaver relish all winter.

Yes, balm of Gilead! The tree of life for all seasons. The tree of life that supports all those who share its wild world. The tree of life that uplifts a solitary man on this spring morning.

I walked on, excited, renewed, energetic, and yet at rest. This hour's quiet moments had been carved out of a hectic schedule, to remain enshrined in my memory for years to come. All of it was without cost, without money, and without stress or strain. Some of the most precious moments come in the most unplanned ways.

The air warmed quickly under the touch of April sunshine. It surprised me to see a very large, very fat, and very elegant squirrel scurry into the under brush. He was obviously not one of our common western red squirrels. He was an exotic import. How did he ever come to this remote spit of land? Intriguing indeed!

A little farther on I found a poplar fallen in the lake. The beavers had been busy here. Snow white limbs stripped clean of their sweet bark lay in the water. I picked one up. It was exactly the right length, the right thickness, and the right heft to fit me as a perfect walking stick. It felt familiar at once. It would accompany me on a hundred walks across the hills.

"Oh happy day!" I hummed to myself. "Yes, Oh happy day!"

What a bonus the balm of Gilead bestowed on me.

No wonder, no wonder, Christ Himself is also called *The Balm of Gilead.*

Wild Geese

The soul-stirring sound drifted down to earth, to the valley bottom, and to the depths of my being. Wild geese on wing again! Wild, strong-winged wonders of the wilderness. Headed north, for the far reaches of the Arctic tundra, still at least two thousand miles away. Already the fearless travelers of the sky's highways had crossed half a continent from the southern marshes, lakes, and waterways of southern California.

In quiet awe, face upturned, I listened to the haunting cries that had carried across the countryside for uncounted thousands of years. Rooted to the same spot high on a wild ridge, I was lost in reassuring wonder at the realization that some of our most memorable moments have an eternal dimension of enduring quality to them. The bugle notes of the geese, serenading an outdoor man, were an annual spring symphony playing at full fortissimo, free for anyone to relish. It was a strong, sudden reminder that some things in our ever changing scene do endure.

Yes, for the few moments of their passing, I was again reassured that our Father, designer of all things wild and free, not only sustained this species, but me as well. He only, and He alone, remained ever the same, unchanging, and eternally trustworthy in a universe where all else was change. And in that intense, burning awareness came great good cheer and quiet consolation. "*I am the same. I change not!*" What glorious assurance amid such a troubled, torn, and unpredictable world scene.

The geese were traveling at a tremendous speed. Looking out across the greening valley I carefully compared their rate of progress with the speeding traffic, northbound, on the main mountain highway headed for Alaska. The flight of the handsome, dark-winged birds easily surpassed the velocity of the fastest vehicles roaring up the road at sixty miles an hour. The long wavering V's of geese gave the impression of undulating waves soaring in gentle motion against the clouds. In reality, pushed by a strong tail wind, they were hurtling through the air at seventy miles an hour.

And the astonishing miracle so seldom even considered by careless people below was that this incredible pace would be maintained hour after hour, from dawn to dusk. Great tendons, powerful wing muscles charged with oxygen from the thin high atmosphere drawn by heaving chests and laboring lungs, would propel the wild ones like projectiles through space, dead on course. All of this without computers, without micro-chip processors or any of the other gadgetry of which humans bray with endless pride.

For me as a common man, uncomplicated by sophistication, this acute realization swept over my awareness in an intense sense of utter humiliation. Though so late in life, the spectacle of the wild geese in full flight made me freshly aware of what Christ fully meant on that memorable day when He taught on the mount. "*Look at the birds in the sky! They never sow, nor reap nor store away in barns, and yet your heavenly Father feeds them! Aren't you more precious to Him than they are?*" (*Matthew 6:26* PHILLIPS).

It was a poignant, piercing question.
It pulled me up short.
It was an arrow within!

The wild skeins of geese in full flight had caught my attention. Stopped dead in my tracks while in full stride, they had turned my thoughts to eternal issues. This was a moving moment in one man's life.

Did my life in action, in full view, and under sudden observation from onlookers actually attract people's attention to Christ? Was there some quality of enduring worth and eternal value to my coming and going that turned another's thoughts toward God, my Father? Would someone pause and give quiet thanks that somehow God's gracious Spirit would arrange for me to sweep across their horizon, if only for a few passing moments.

When the geese were gone—enveloped in a distant haze, I bowed my head and in utter stillness of spirit prayed softly, *"Oh Father, make the moments of my life count for you! Always."*

Bountiful Blossoms

L ast evening a gentle, insistent, warm rain saturated the whole landscape. Everything everywhere that grows from our rocky ridges and rolling rangelands is turning emerald green. The transformation lasts only a few short, pulsing weeks in spring. It is a glorious transition time from the stark whiteness of winter months to the severe and stern bronze of hot summer seasons.

But it is an interval of breathtaking beauty.
The blue skies are reflected in turquoise blue lakes.
White, bright cumulous clouds climb above the mountains.
A soft skene of green foliage covers the countryside.
The hill slopes of green parkland glow with the golden swatches of wild balsam root in full flower.
And scattered far and wide beneath the red-barked ponderosa pines are the lovely ola-llas.

This year there is an abundance of bloom unmatched for at least half a century in this verdant valley. Seldom in one man's lifetime is there such a prolifigate show of wild glory.

The olalla bushes in particular defy description. One must actually see them firsthand, caught up in silent wonder and sincere gratitude for so much splendor.

The olalla bushes vary in size from that of a small rose bush clinging tenaciously to a tough rock outcrop to giant vase-shaped shrubs twenty feet tall, growing luxuriously in some rich soil in a sheltered spot. The multi-stemmed bushes with their delicate lacework of slim limbs bow and bend in the breeze. And this spring every twig from top to bottom bears a pulsing profusion of snow white blossoms. So brilliant is their brightness that even a mile away they appear as white puffs of fresh popcorn scattered at random across the green hills.

There are olallas all around us. Not one was ever planted by the hand of man. Their seeds strike root wherever the birds, or bears, or even the canny coyotes, decide to drop their dung. They are a wonder to the eyes, a wild joy to the spirit.

Last evening on a sudden impulse, despite the dripping dampness, I decided to go out and walk in the rain. It was just getting dusk. Everywhere I walked the olallas hung heavy with moisture. Every leaf, every twig, every blossom was turgid with moisture. And in the soft evening air the elusive, faint perfume of the wild blossoms permeated the atmosphere all around me. Even though it was dusk and almost dark I strolled softly through the late twilight lost in quiet contentment and the gentle peace of the moment.

To my surprise I saw a humming bird hovering over the white flowers, feeding on their rich nectar so late at night! Then came the great giant moths drawn by the sweet and delicate perfume. Then came a solitary man who paused long enough to draw the abundant blossoms to his face, inhaling deeply of their fragrance in the rain.

In that instant of time there swept into my soul an acute and amazing awareness of a profound, eternal principle. All of this beauty, all of these gorgeous blooms, and all of this exquisite fragrance had emerged from a realm that endured the toughest winter of this century. *Out of adversity comes beauty!*

Month after month, beginning in early autumn last year, this valley had lain in the grip of a harsh, hard winter. Storms, unrelenting storms of sleet and ice and snow, swept over the land. Plunging temperatures that broke all records with below freezing, chill readings locked the trees and shrubs and plants in cruel cold. Sometimes one wondered if they could survive.

But they did! The coming of spring was akin to the arrival of another miracle of renewal, of rebirth, and of resurrection. For out of the desperate depths of winter weather came new life, abundant life, and bountiful blossoms of remarkable beauty.

Our Father has the wondrous capacity to just do that for us!

He can turn the toughest times into days of pure delight.

He actually does make all things new. He makes them bright and beautiful as well. He has a way of turning trials into triumphs. What joy!

I strolled home softly through the deepening darkness.

Small droplets of moisture spattered on my dear, old Stetson.

There was something very soothing in the sound.

Dark, damp drops of rain fell from the clouds, from the overhanging pines to moisten my warm jacket.

But inside I was snug, warm, and at peace.

My boots scuffed through wet grass.

It was all so reassuring.

Nothing spectacular.

Nothing sensational.

Nothing staggering.

Just a solitary soul in intimate interaction with a gentle moment of divine renewal in the earth. An ordinary man finding refreshment of mind in the twilight of a spring evening. A searching spirit drinking deeply from the fountain of God's gracious grace and goodness all around him.

The lights beckoned me to come back. They glowed gold through the evening mist and moisture. How blessed I was to have this snug shelter from the rain. I turned my steps toward home in quiet contentment.

But within my innermost being there lingered an even more profound peace. The peace that comes clearly and calmly to the person who truly knows Christ. It is He who assures us that He conveys to us a peace more profound than any arranged in the world by human ingenuity.

It is the wondrous peace of His own presence.

It is in His presence with me that I sense and know assuredly that all will be well no matter what challenges come. No matter how desperate some days may be, He, and only He, can bring bountiful blessings out of the bareness.

If He can produce beautiful blossoms out of wild winter weather, surely, surely He can bring great glory out of my grim, gray days.

He is here. He is near. He is dear indeed. So all is well!

Thoughts on Tulips

B ecause the wild deer on our hills took such a fancy to our flowers, only a scraggly remnant of tulips managed to bloom. At best they were only a tiny handful, struggling against the trampling of hooves and nibbling of eager lips.

Then last week, suddenly, joyously, a dear little neighbor lady stood at our door, bringing us a glorious bouquet of perfect tulips. What a generous gesture of goodwill. Her garden only a few short doors from us is never touched by the deer. Perhaps because a great, golden Labrador dog patrols the property.

Anyway, the fire-engine red tulips decorating our home have brought with them enormous pleasure. Not just because they are a gentle reminder of a kind and caring friend, but also because they are a remarkable creation of pure perfection. We had only one bloom in the garden of comparable beauty. But both Ursula and I stood and gazed into its flaming heart with quiet wonder.

No doubt the bulbs from which these flowers came originated in Holland, thousands of miles across the chill, gray, fog shrouded North Atlantic. But looking into the scarlet cups of the tulips on our table is akin to looking into the sacred chalice of a wild, wind-blown poppy off the foothills of the Himalayas in Pakistan.

So intense is the red, so incandescent with fire when touched by the sun, that it glows hot. As the petals open there is a mysterious pool of black ink gathered at the heart of the flower. . . perhaps the closest color to pure black found anywhere in nature. For black in essence is the total absence of light. But this pool of jet black color radiates light, shimmering and silken smooth. And most marvelous of all it is fringed with an intricate and ornate band of the most golden gold. No wonder ancient temples were ornamented with the most dazzling colors in startling combinations.

The ideas and inspiration and indulgence came from the wild flowers of the fields that Christ called us to look at long and carefully. Our tulips opened wider and wider in unabashed glory. From tip to tip the glowing petals spread wide more than six inches across, shouting for attention and co-mingled adoration.

Never before in all my seventy-three years had I ever given so much close contemplation to any bloom. Every part was elegant, serene, and superbly designed. Out of the black pool at its center emerged a pale green pistil surmounted with an intricate crown of pure gold. Surrounding this special pedestal stood a circle of black stamens as straight and erect as an honor guard of troopers surrounding their monarch.

Suddenly there burst in upon my contemplation the awareness of standing in the presence of a humble tulip that bore itself in regal splendor. Here was beauty of design that demanded deep respect. Here was a combination of colors in exquisite artistry. Here was a delicacy of pure delight to the eyes and uplift to a man's spirit . . . all arranged in loving care by my Father.

And in that instant I whispered softly, sincerely to my wife who was beside me, "And to think so much beauty could burst out of the rough brown bulb planted in quiet faith last fall!" For a few moments there was utter silence, quiet stillness between us. Then the words tumbled from my soul without pretence or premeditation, "And still people don't believe in our Father's majestic miracles!"

Swiftly in rapid succession the thoughts tumbled out of
me.
So much beauty, yet so much unbelief.
So much splendor, yet so much cynicism.
So much perfection, yet so much perversion.

Everywhere on every side, around us, above us, in the skies,
beneath our feet in the soil, in trees and shrubs, in grass and
flowers, in birds on wing, and in insects in the sun a million
miracles are made in silence and perfection. Each for a purpose.
Each with meticulous design. Each with wondrous beauty.

Yet men and women, with awful arrogance, bray, "There
is no God!" Blinded by their own belligerence against the generosity of our Father, they cannot see His wondrous work in the
earth, nor see His love in all He touches in the cosmos.

But I look into the heart of a flaming tulip and see the
glory of His grace to me.

The White Clover

W hen we first came to live in this home, perched high on its rocky ridge, I was a bit daunted by the rough ground on three sides of the home. In order to build a strong, sturdy structure in this tough location overlooking the lovely lake below, massive blasting of the bed rock had to be done for the basement. So tons of broken rock, shards of stone, and accumulated debris from the excavation surrounded the house on three sides.

Here all sorts of tough weeds such as the native tumbleweed, wild mustard, couch grass, and mullen had taken root. It was an unsightly conglomeration of wild growth that posed a fire hazard so close to the house. Trying to eradicate the weeds on such rough terrain was a challenge that demanded a great deal of heavy handwork every growing season.

It was a knotty problem to know what might be best to do with such a difficult site where growing anything desirable or delightful to the eye would be impossible. Then one day in a sudden flash of reflection I remembered seeing wild white clover flourishing in the rocky hills on tough terrain. The seed had been dropped there in the dung of some deer or steer. Yet, unaided by any human help the sturdy plants had spread a carpet of green glory over the rocky ground. Maybe the same could happen around our home on the hill.

In vain I searched for seed of this humble, hardy little plant that was so perseverant in its growth on rough ground. Then one day, almost as a last ditch effort, a seed supplier offered to bring in some wild white clover seed from New Zealand, half a world away. In co-mingled excitement and serious doubt if the exotic clover would even survive in our severe climate, I decided to give it a chance.

With loving care and quiet faith the fine, fine seed, as minute as fine-ground pepper, was sown broadcast over the broken, rocky ground. The seeds were so small I was sure even the birds would scarcely notice them enough to pick them up. Then I waited, waited—waited for weeks and weeks. It seemed ages!

As fall approached and the weather grew cooler, I began to notice here and there delicate touches of tender green began to appear amongst the broken shards of stone. But by now surely it was too late in the season for the tender new plants to make it. I was mistaken—the cool rainy days of November, the chill nights, seemed to suit the clover. Perhaps the season was akin to spring in its native New Zealand. By the time hard winter weather arrived a thin mat of greenery covered large areas of the tough terrain. But how would the clover come through a rugged Canadian winter? And last winter was to be one of the most severe of this century.

To my unbounded joy the white clover came to full life in a burst of extraordinary spring growth. Everywhere its roots were running out rapidly to cover new ground. And now a carpet of emerald-green growth covers the unsightly accumulation of broken rock and barren soil. It astonishes me to no end! It has exceeded my wildest expectations! Today it is a carpet of white blossoms.

Often, often, often as I stand quietly and look upon this lovely, luxuriant growth I am reminded of the ancient adage: *Just glow, wherever you grow.* No big deal. Just calmly be faithful, fruitful, and full of goodwill wherever our Father sees fit to plant us for a spell.

The terrain may be very tough, the growing conditions very uncongenial, the days very desperate, and the going very grim!

But if the humble, hardy white clover can carpet the rock shards around my house with its gentle, green glory, surely my simple life can be used by the Master to cover over some of the tough spots in my sordid society. We are told very clearly in unmistakable language, *"Be not overcome with evil—but overcome evil with good."*

The dynamic, overcoming life of the clover has done just this. So too the divine, dynamic life of the Living Christ at work in me can overcome all adversities around me. He says plainly, *"In this world you shall have tribulation (troubles), but be of good cheer; I have (and can) overcome the world" (John 16:33).*

Spring Runoff

Two days ago I stood beside a mountain cascade in full flood. At least ten months of the year this small stream is just that, a thin rivulet of water flowing gently over its rocky bed of granite boulders. Its song is not much more than a muted melody, the sounds of its movements a soft murmuring.

But this week of spring runoff with a fierce sun stripping the winter snow from the high country, the gentle stream has become charged with enormous energy and power. A literal torrent of ice-cold water is roaring over the rocks, rushing down the valley to spill into the lake. From there it will eventually reach the mighty Columbia and finally empty into the open waters of the Pacific.

As I stood beside the surging current, immersed in calm contemplation of the majestic power and volume of its waters, a clear, pensive, piercing thought came to me. *It just can't keep this gigantic flow to itself!* Its flood waters would touch nearly six hundred miles of diverse terrain along the long winding course of its trek to the sea.

Its snow-fed waters would help fill the glorious mountain lakes of our mountain valley. It would ultimately flow through at least four of these, besides the great reaches of the Columbia.

All along its course its rich flow would be home to hundreds of species of birds and mammals, fish and reptiles. Everything from wild geese, grebes, beavers, muskrats, otters, trout and turtles would relish its life. *No, it just can't keep the flow to itself!*

All along its torturous route a thousand pumps would draw its delicious refreshment from the lakes and rivers to irrigate the desert. Huge orchards of apples, pears, peaches, and plums lived because of it. Hay fields, livestock pastures, and gigantic gardens all flourished because it came. *No, it just can't keep the flow to itself!*

Its rushing waters would thunder through huge turbines, turning its energy into electrical power that ran across the dry desert country for hundreds of miles. It generated enough energy to light a thousand homes. *It just can't keep the flow to itself!*

From the innermost sanctum of my spirit, almost unconsciously, yet with wrenching earnestness, a simple sentence request rose to God. *"May the outflow of Your life, surging through my soul, never be kept to myself!"* Its very expression, uttered in stunning sincerity, astonished me.

> It was an intense truth.
>> It was seen in brittle clarity—cutting through all confusion.
>> Christ's abundant, surging life touches me, transforms me,
>>> Then pours out to impact a thousand others along my trail.

"I just can't keep the flow to myself."
> It must be passed on gladly.
> It must be shared freely.
> It must be spread widely.

Hummingbird Evening

I t was a warm, gentle, still, late spring evening. Already the sun, now setting far to the northwest over the ragged ranges, was tinting the whole world with a mellow golden glow. It was an interlude of palpable peace and repose.

My friend and I sat on the hand-laid, rough, stone wall that surrounds my patio. We were two special friends in deep discussion about the dreaded disease that now darkened the horizon of my companion's entire life and career. Would the suspected killer cut short his days? Was there still hope for the future? Could a ray of hope still penetrate the inner deepening darkness? Only our Father's care could compensate for the crisis he faced.

We sat in silence—as good friends do—speaking hardly at all, communing spirit to spirit in our shared sorrow. At such moments too much talk can be trivial—a torment. So we were still, pensive in this poignant evening setting. The warm air was redolent with the pungent perfume of the native greasewood in full bloom around the patio.

Suddenly, swiftly, shattering the solitude, a gallant male hummingbird hurtled out of the sky in a spectacular power dive. He shot past us only a few feet from our faces, then paused in full flight to hover steadily in midair before a greasewood bush

in front of us. There sat his mate not more than two and one-half inches long, weighing only a couple of ounces. *A calliope hummingbird*—the smallest of these small bird species found on this continent. . . a native of our western mountains.

The little gladiator was in the surging throes of his own nuptial flight. In an instant he applied full power to his whirring wings and shot straight up in vertical flight with an incredible display of aerial acrobatics. The most advanced military aircraft in all the world could not begin to match his maneuvers from hovering dead still in midair to a sudden upward power climb like a rocket off a launch pad in instant full flight.

We sat there stunned, speechless, shocked, and spellbound.

Again and again and again the hummer carried out his courting display. It was as if his entire tiny body was a dynamic projectile of flesh and feathers, blood and bone, that blazed hot with enormous energy. The swift rush of his flight up and down, up and down through the quiet calm of the evening, transfixed all of our attention. Here before us was a bundle of brilliant feathers and whirring wings that could easily be held in the span of a child's hand. Yet bound up within that tiny body were powers of flight and endurance that eclipsed any engine ever designed by the ingenuity of human engineers or aircraft designers.

Because my friend had been in the Royal British Air Force during World War II, he was more than familiar with all types of combat aircraft. So for him in particular this was an interlude of enormous impact upon his shadowed spirit. In a new and tangible sense, *"He had seen the glory of the Lord."* The wonder of Christ our Creator had once again been displayed before him in the fantastic flight of a tiny little hummingbird at the edge of the desert and at the edge of flight!

When the twilight closed in quietly around us, it was as if both of us men had been enfolded in the calm consolation of our Father's care. The sublime assurance which swept over my own soul was, *If He can provide the power and the impetus to sustain this remarkable species upon the planet, so, too, can He provide for me and my friend in this dire ordeal.* To use a well-known phrase, *"It was an hour of power."*

Out of this hour, so unplanned, so spontaneous, and so calmly arranged by our loving Father there had come new life, new excitement, new joy, new delight, and new vitality.

That is just the way it is with God!
Christ our Friend is here to help, to heal, and to hearten.
Even if it is in something as small as a tiny bird.
Christ Himself said, *"Behold the birds of the air."*

We had, we had! My friend turned to me calmly, his eyes all aglow, and said, "Phillip, I shall never, ever forget this evening!"

Ten days later:
Our front room was filled with unexpected visitors. Suddenly the phone rang. Ursula left the room to answer it. A few moments later she returned, her face radiant with joy. "Rich (my friend facing the dread disease) called to tell us the most wonderful news!" she exclaimed.

He had been in to have a further examination and major consultation with the specialist. And to the surgeon's absolute astonishment the threatening condition had gone into complete remission. There was no medical explanation for the reversal. Even the technicians who carried out the scan were amazed beyond belief at the radical change.

The surgeon without skepticism had said, "This is a miracle!" To which my humble friend replied quietly, "Sir, you may be sure God, our Father, had something to do with this! There were those of us who trusted Him."

All of us in the front room were so jubilant with joy we could scarcely restrain ourselves. In a gesture of profound gratitude to God, I raised my right arm in a royal salute and declared aloud, "THANK YOU, FATHER!"

The next day my friend's wife called to give me further details of the entire interview with the specialist. Then she added softly, "Phillip, my husband used to get so tired, so easily spent, and so quickly worn-out and exhausted. Now he just goes and goes and goes with amazing energy."

"Yes," I mused to myself silently, "Almost as much energy as a hummingbird in full flight."

It was my Master—Christ my Friend, who said it best, *"Look at the birds flying around; they do not plant seeds; gather a harvest and put it in barns; yet your Father in heaven takes care of them. Aren't you worth much more than birds? Can any of you live a bit longer by worrying about it?"*

Instead some of us just trust Him to care for us. He does!

Mountain Vespers

Two days ago I was in a high, wild, wilderness terrain absolutely new to me. Such interludes still thrill my spirit, in part because I tramp the high country fully alert, eagerly exposed to all the nuances of the natural environment around me. The mountains just do supply me with an enormous uplift both physically and spiritually. This inspiration is a generous gift bestowed in intimacy by my Father as we walk the woods and the high country together.

It had rained most of the morning. But in the afternoon the clouds began to blow into oblivion. By evening the whole earth pulsed with a golden glow. Just then I came upon a forest setting of such serene splendor that ordinary human language is scarcely able to describe it adequately. But I must try in order to share the impact of the place with others.

A gentle open glade of several thousand acres nestled securely between two rock ridges lay bathed in warm sunshine. The entire meadow was a brilliant, sparkling green valley. Because of the moisture adorning every blade of grass, every leaf on plants and herbs, the vegetation pulsed with a gleaming radiance reflecting the setting sun. It was as if ten million points of light were lit for evening vespers.

Scattered in random beauty across the green meadow stood

the most magnificent assortment of ponderosa pines and western mountain larch I had ever seen in my whole life. The scene
stopped me in full stride. Seldom, seldom, seldom does one ever
see such a stand of superb specimens at full maturity in the
warm loveliness of their rich, copper-colored bark.

At full growth both species are tremendous, tall trees reaching almost two hundred feet into the thin mountain air. Unlike
the gigantic Douglas firs, redwoods and Sitka spruce of the west
coast, which grow in dense, heavily shaded forests, these open,
sun-loving, sun-drenched, sun-kissed trees stood tall and stately
on the green sward like the giant pillars of a cathedral.

I was utterly awestruck with the scene. I stood in subdued
silence.

The most gifted landscape gardener could not have arranged a more glorious masterpiece. This one had been planted
by God Himself and tended only with His tender, consummate
care for hundreds of seasons. Why the roaring, tearing teeth of
chain saws and the grinding, gouging growls of bulldozers had
not torn the soul out of this sanctuary astonished me. Perhaps
one reason it had been preserved from the cruel clutch of man
was my Father who hoped it would touch and lift and quicken
the souls of a few mountain men like myself who fiercely love
the wild and unspoiled places.

I stood in reverence. I stood in awe. I stood in wonder. For
at least fifty years I had searched for the supreme stand of
ponderosas and larch to photograph in a pristine setting. This
evening my quest was complete. What a find! What a treasure!
I took picture after picture, somehow profoundly aware that
nothing on film could ever fully convey the ambience, the pure
atmosphere, or the afterglow of the hour.

The tall towering trees of such rich, red hue stood out in
sharp contrast to the verdant green all around and beneath them.
To walk amongst them softly was to stroll under the colonnades
of a colossal cathedral in the high country. These were moments suspended in time but also suspended forever in my
memory of greater worth than any gold.

Softly, sincerely, almost in adoration, I ran my rough hands
over the sun-warmed bark of the sturdy trunks. Those of the

larch were relatively smooth, sheathed in long slender strands of copper-colored bark. The ponderosa pines had giant slabs of rich red bark interspersed with a network of dark, almost-black grooves. Many painters and photographers consider this the most beautiful tree bark in all the earth. This evening it pulsed with pure, primitive, power, untouched, unmarred by any man.

Quietly, calmly, convincingly, the awareness enfolded my soul that I had been the recipient of a tremendous treasure this twilight hour.

Beneath my rough bush boots I was amazed to discover such a variety of grasses, plants, herbs, and wild flowers growing lavishly in their prolific plant community. Because of the high altitude some were only just ready to burst into bloom. But there were mountain daisies, wild columbine, native violets, wild strawberries, and a score of other species ready to scent the air and tint the greensward with their blooms. I almost hesitated to walk anywhere less I desecrate the sod. I was indeed treading on sacred soil, as sublime as any floor covering in any sanctuary.

I had decided to spend the night there, curled up in a couple of old, well-worn blankets. As the sun settled beyond the sawtooth skyline to the west, the high mountain robins began their evening serenade. It blended into the melody of a small stream that murmured softly through the glade. Then, just then, several vesper sparrows added their pure, plaintive vesper calls to the soft evening song. If ever there was in truth a vesper service of primitive purity, this was it, played out in absolute innocence for all eternity.

For a mountain man, well into the late twilight of his own earth sojourn, this interlude stands out with glowing delight and sheer ecstasy which no pen can possibly portray on paper. I had entered a celestial cathedral of divine design. In truth this had been for me hallowed ground. And in that place of supreme peace I had again encountered the person of Christ Himself who as He assured us, *"Goes ahead to prepare places of supreme serenity for us."* Not just in the next world, but in this one as well.

The sharp night air intensified the aroma of the pines and flowering plants. Their co-mingled perfume enfolded me in my blankets. I sighed deeply with undisguised delight and gratitude for such a glorious evening. What a privileged person I was!

Just then a pair of coyotes called from the ridge above me. It could not have been a more fond farewell. I dozed off to sleep. All was well!

Granite

The gigantic ridges and rugged ranges of our mountain region have a unique quality of strength and grandeur to them. In part this is because of the open, sun-splashed terrain where mountain meadows, park-like forests, and giant slabs of gray granite are interspersed. The towering, rough, high country is not just an attractive delight to the eye, but also a marvelous region in which to roam freely, lost in quiet meditation, yet challenged to climb hard.

One has to pull on sturdy hiking boots and a rough bush jacket, then go out and plant their feet on the lofty crags to know this land firsthand. It is not enough to merely admire the mountains from afar.

I do it again and again and again. There simply is no substitute for firsthand encounters utterly alone with the granite rock that soars to the sky. You must meet it in intimate contact to respect its grandeur and to be stirred by its enduring strength and might.

Yesterday I did just that . . . perhaps for the hundredth time, I climbed a new ridge on a different range which is still all part of my beloved high country. It is a rare pleasure to have so much wild country so close to my door, so much a part of my "world." As I stood on the summit of gray granite, the same, special, sweet sensation of utter stillness swept over me in wave upon wave of inspiration. Only the wild, wilderness cry of a jet black raven on wing pierced the solitude, giving even deeper poignancy to the moment.

Co-mingled storm clouds and giant thunderheads magnified the mountain majesty. It was as if I stood in awe alone in the throne room of the Most High with wide vistas sweeping away in every segment of the scene. I could see for miles and miles and miles. Ranches and roads and open range lay open like tiny patches of paintwork on a giant masterpiece spread out beneath my feet.

As I gazed in wonder, a startling, shattering, shaking thought swept through my innermost being. It was as if in an instant of time for but a moment in eternity this common man was beholding the earth through the eyes of God Himself. Put another way, suddenly it seemed my Father had given me His own personal perspective on life.

And the searching questions that shot through my awareness were something like this—quickened by His presence—ignited by His Spirit.

"These mountains endure millennium upon millennium. I your Lord God also endure forever. Why then do you ever fret or fear? I am ever here! Yet your race struggles and strains, caught up completely in the tiny transient tensions of trying to survive. It is so much better just to trust me."

I stood there subdued, silent, with nothing to say.

I gazed out at the hairlike lines that were winding roads—at the tiny dots that were houses, barns, and odd buildings—at the minute patchwork of fields and meadows—where men and women worried and worked and wore themselves away in toil and tears. I had done that, too, for years. Yes, for hard, harsh years before I came to Christ and cast the whole of my life into His care.

He had assured me then, as He still does to this very hour, "Give me all of yourself—and I will give you all of Myself." And I did—I turned all of my life, my mind, my interests, my will, my possessions, my pursuits, my hopes, and my future to Him. In exchange He has given me His own glorious life in abundant measure, year upon year.

It was, and is, and always will be through close, personal, firsthand encounter. It is in knowing Him, trusting Him.

Momentarily I glanced down at the rugged gray granite below my rough boots. I loved it with a life long passion. The rugged rock had always been the high road to the high country. No wonder the ancient poet declared with delight, *"He is my high rock."*

Butter-and-Eggs

Butter-and-eggs—a most unusual name for a most attractive wildflower. So named because of the brilliant yellow and orange colors co-mingled in their blossoms. The intense, bright, glorious flowers are visible at great distances, no matter how drab or barren the desert soil is where they grow in wild and joyous abandon.

They are not a native species to North America. Some homesick early settlers brought their seed from the homeland in Europe. Now centuries later their species has spread clear across the continent. And in my candid estimation they stand tall, erect, sturdy, and lovely with the finest of our native flora.

Butter-and-eggs have become one of the most arresting plants in our dry desert terrain. Their glory lasts for weeks and weeks. They thrive on barren soil, hot cut banks, and stony ground. They make no demands on man for their care and attention. The lovely blossoms only seek some wasteland on which to flourish and bloom in wild abundance.

Every spring I make a habit of going out to gather several armfuls as beautiful bouquets for our home. The hardy, erect stems with their bright blossoms are pure delight in any room. They just simply adorn any setting with gentle good cheer. Best of all they last and last for days and days.

As I strolled home the other evening, bearing my bouquet of golden glory, a compelling thought gripped my mind. We, as God's people, really ought to be just like butter-and-eggs. Just exotics in a setting of strange soil in a strange land in a strange society. Asking no special care, no special place, or no special concessions. Seeking only the chance to bloom and flourish in some tough terrain where others can't endure.

If that is where Christ, the Master Gardener, wants us to grow and shed some of His splendor on the scene, why not? He said we were to be light in the world. Let's just do it!

Sudden Surprises

I t has been a spring season filled to capacity with a wide assortment of responsibilities: teaching classes every week in a town fifty miles from home, working steadily on this book manuscript, sharing in the suffering and sorrow of dear friends facing death, carrying on a colossal correspondence with people all over the continent, plus all the demands of caring for the grounds and garden around our home.

Then the other day, in her genial, gentle way, Ursula whispered to me, "Darling, why don't you just slip away into the hills for a few hours!? The break from all your work will do you great good! You really deserve a change!"

Wonderful words from a lovely lady. In a matter of minutes I had pulled on heavy socks and boots, slipped into my bush jacket, grabbed my faded old Stetson, and headed for the hills. Happily they rise in wild terrain just across the road from us. In two minutes time I was climbing steadily across glorious open parkland still largely in its pristine condition.

I had not been in these hills so familiar to me for several months. The lush growth of spring, the unusual intermittent rains, and the warm weather between showers had combined to create the impression I was in a luxuriant tropical setting. Even as I hiked, rain drops spattered on the ancient Stetson from cool, scattered clouds. Everything sparkled with moisture, and I could move through the scene in utter silence.

What a perfect day for outdoor adventures.

The first surprise was to come to a barren rock slide which in former years had pulsed with heat from the summer sun. Here, suddenly, to my unbounded delight, it was decorated with a wild sprinkling of vivid scarlet buglers in full bloom. They are one of the dainty tough plants that take root in tough terrain. The sight astonished me. The red splash of crimson color adorned the whole slope. At the foot of the slide a fine stand of fireweed blazed bright, the first I had ever seen there.

In joyous praise I gave thanks to my Father for such beauty, so unexpected in such an unlikely location.

My legs seemed to take on new energy, carrying me up a deer trail into heavy timber. This is where the does withdraw with their spotted fawns to shelter from the sun. I moved as stealthily as a wraith of mist through the forest, hoping to find a doe in repose.

Suddenly, instead, there was the soft "swoosh" of large dark wings lifting off a branch just above my head. A huge horned owl had been resting in the dense tangle of intertwined willows. I watched him float through the trees in soft, soaring flight. It was the closest encounter I ever had with these fierce hunters of the northern woods.

Normally by this late season they have long ago left for the north. Surprise, surprise! What a special day this was already. What beautiful bonuses had been bestowed on me.

Soon I broke out above the heavy timber into glorious, open, grassy glades carpeted with an abundant array of wildflowers. It seemed hardly another human had hiked these hills for weeks. I sensed that somehow the wild places and my wild friends of hoof, wing, and paw were welcoming me back. I stopped to rest on the crest of a giant rock outcrop. The whole mountain realm cradling the lake spread out below like an aerial photo. The red-tiled roof of my home stood out sharply against the greenery. And in the stillness I deeply breathed in refreshment of soul, inspiration of spirit, and renewed strength of body.

How few enjoyed rare interludes of this sort so close to home within rifle shot of one's own front door! What an honor.

I started to descend when a gorgeous blue grouse flew up from my feet and lit quickly on a gray ridge of granite less than fifty feet away. To my surprise, the beautiful big bird did not take flight in fear. Instead, the proud cock, with low clucks, strutted his stuff in full view of me. I crouched low to the ground to set him at ease. In moments he was again "Master of the Mountain." I grinned in glee and sheer exultation.

We spent a long spell together—we two wild wanderers of the high hills. By the time we parted we were utterly at peace and quietly contented in this gentle encounter, just two old friends together again for a spell.

The afternoon was wearing on. It was time to head for home. But instead of taking the shortest trail down, I felt an inner constraint to swing out wide over an open ridge where I had not tramped for months and months. It was ablaze with an unbelievable array of wildflowers, as glorious as any of the high alpine meadows of the great mountains. All of this was so close to home, so free for the taking, and so abundant in beauty and fragrance. Yet most of our people had simply never taken the time or trouble or strength to search out this special spot.

As I pushed my way through a small stand of young pines, a magnificent mule deer doe burst from her bed. She was a superb specimen, every muscle tense and taut, every movement agile and graceful. With enormous bounds, bursting with energy, she cleared the open ground in a flash of time. Her rich, red summer coat stood out in sharp contrast to the greenery all around us. Her departure was a heart-pounding demonstration of pure power in motion. I had seen it scores and scores of times before in my wild wanderings across the world.

Still, its splendor, its spirit, and its surge of sudden energy left me spellbound. Only my Creator, the living Christ, could create a creature of such grace and glory. As her hoofbeats died away in the distance I knew assuredly that this day had been rich, rich, rich with sudden surprises. Each was a beautiful bonus bestowed on me in gracious generosity by God, my Father.

As I rambled home, the weariness of the morning melted away. In His mercy and kindness my living Lord and Friend had renewed my youth like an eagle's. How dear He is!

Leaves, Leaves, Leaves

To look at, it is a lovely tree. Ever since the first day I set eyes on this property, the handsome, young cherry tree just outside the breakfast nook aroused admiration. In spring and in summer its thick, dense foliage was a sight to behold—leaves, leaves, leaves.

The new, tender branches grew at a prodigious pace. The tree seemed so healthy, so robust, and so vigorous; it was virtually immune to the ravages of insects or disease. Without the use of chemical sprays or insecticides it just stood strong in the sun and burgeoned into leaves, leaves, leaves.

Season after season we have waited patiently for its snow-white blossoms to set fruit. Few, few ever did. Last summer only a few small handfuls of stunted fruit came off this imposing tree. And this year there will be almost none to even taste. But leaves, leaves, leaves are everywhere.

Next week when all the other garden work is done, the cherry tree will come down, cut to the ground, cut off at the roots, cut off in the full but false display of its green glory. Only leaves, leaves, leaves!

A strong, sturdy but sweet-fruited apricot will replace it. Not half as handsome, only half as tall, but twice as productive. It is fruit we want, not just a show.

In quiet, pensive moments, working in the deep shade of that spreading, green-leaved tree, I have come to understand clearly what Christ meant when He uttered the simple words, *"For the tree is known by his fruit!"* —not by its appearance, not by its imposing size, not by its vigorous growth, and not by its abundant leaves, leaves, leaves.

Put in the most basic terms, all that counts is fruit.
What is true for the cherry tree is likewise true for me.
A show, a sham, or empty splendor just doesn't count.
Instead, the Master Gardener comes looking for fruit. The sweet fruit of His own character, His own conduct, and His own consecration made real in me!!

Wings of Mercy

Our lawn is not large or imposing. It was put in to help soften the harsh contours and rock-girt terrain of the ridge on which the house was built. When first we came, it was infected with weeds and riddled with insects, which did great damage to its well-being.

Bit by bit, year by year, the weeds were slowly suppressed. And as the grass began to flourish, so did the wild birds that moved in to take over the green sward as their feeding and hunting territory.

Several days ago in a gentle interlude of repose, I sat in the sun at the edge of the lawn and quietly watched my winged friends at work. A pair of barn swallows and a pair of fly catchers had both laid claim to the lawn.

It astonished me to see the speed and deftness with which the wild ones swooped over the grass plucking insects out of the air in full flight. The gray moths, which ruin so many lawns, were eradicated in swift pursuit. Often the fly catchers would hover over a single spot then drop down to seize their quarry in the thick turf.

Wings of mercy, wings of benefit, wings of help in time of need. The thought made me pause and reflect on our Father's mercy for us, the guardian angels He has provided for His people.

Often, often we are oblivious to their presence, not fully aware of their gentle acts of mercy, insensitive to the protection they provide amid the perils of life. Like so much of our sojourn, we take for granted the goodness and mercy of our God who in His providential ways does make it possible for us to enjoy green pastures and fair meadows.

These are not there just by chance. Rather they flourish and we benefit because of His wings of mercy that hover above the everyday events of our quiet walks with Him.

Thank you, Father, for your gracious, loving care!

Hardy Hollyhock

I stood alone in the late evening light and watched in awe as the fierce gusts of wind bowed and bent the hollyhock bush. It stood alone on the edge of the sun-burned ridge, fully exposed to every blast of air that rushed around it. It stood alone without the shelter of another shrub, tree, or fence to fend off the ferocious winds coming across the hill.

Yet it did not break!
Its tall spikes of beautiful blooms did not crack!
Its proud blossoms flew bravely like flags in battle!

I was enthralled.
Surprise and respect welled up within.
Honor and glory were in the air all around me.

I had no idea where the hollyhock bush came from or how it ever took root in that formidable spot. None of the neighbors have hollyhocks. I have never grown them. They simply are not common in our part of the high country.

But there it was last fall, all alone and seemingly so forlorn. It was struggling to survive on the edge of the wild rangeland just below the house. Cutworms, grasshoppers, and beetles had all attacked it. Still it overcame all the adversities of a tough, cold, biting winter. All I could do was try to protect it with a few handfuls of mulch.

To my unbounded joy it made it through ice, snow, and cutting cold. In spring it put on fresh green foliage. Then as the weather warmed, it shot glorious green spires into the summer sky. At first there were only one or two, then more and more, reaching ever higher. I could not believe a hollyhock could grow to five feet, six feet, yes even seven feet in this sun-blasted, windblown spot.

But it did! And it did it with elan and finesse and great glory. For from its sturdy stems burst blooms of two distinct and delicate colors. One is a passionate purple, the other a rich cream color tinged with pale pink.

How the same bush can produce two types of flowers of divergent hues at the same time remains a mystery to me. Perhaps it is one of those rare hybrids in the plant world that a commercial nursery would pay a fortune to own and propagate. But for me it is a prized possession of even greater worth in the humble lesson of simple steadfastness it has taught me as a man.

Sometimes, our Father, in His infinite wisdom and careful concern, plants us in a tough, wind-blasted spot. It may not be the peaceful place of my choice, the cozy, comfortable corner of my choosing. Yet, bless His name, He sets me there in full view to bring courage, cheer, and sturdy hardiness to those around me.

Again and again and again I have looked at this lone hollyhock and cried out from within, "Oh Christ, by your presence and with your power within, enable me, too, to prevail!"

All of us live in a troubled, stormy society. The raging winds of adversity gust around us with wild abandon. It seems at such times of stress that we cannot stand the strain nor endure the pain. Will we break in the unrelenting "blows" that batter us first in one direction, then in another?

The answer to that sharp question lies within.
It does not have to do with difficult people.
Nor does it depend on cruel circumstances.

The answer lies within the inner sanctum of my soul.

If Christ controls my inner attitudes, all is well.
He alone can give peace amid the pressures of life.

That peace is the power of His own presence.
He, and only He, comprehends the complexities of the hour.
In that assurance lies repose.

It is not for me to try to understand the anguish and stress.
It is not for me to try to explain the evil.
It is not for me to try to vindicate myself.

My part is to stand steadfast in quiet trust in Him who never fails, *and does all things well!!*

Firstfruit

B ecause of a rather cool and unusually rainy season, some of the local fruit has been slow to ripen. But at dawn yesterday I felt a compelling inner urge to go in search of the first apricots, my favorite summer fruit.

I invited my wife to accompany me on this little escapade. We both needed a break from the steady work load of the week. So a wee adventure of this sort could inject real pleasure into our quest. For I love to harvest my own fruit off the tree.

It was a cool, still morning with giant cloud systems climbing the crests of the mountain ranges. The country roads were virtually empty of traffic, and the car cruised along as quietly as a cougar running on rock outcrop.

We were far, far out on remote rangeland when I spotted a lone, wind-blown apricot tree standing sturdy in the corner of a fence by the road. It bore golden fruit. We pulled off onto a patch of gravel, and I hurried over to pick up the first fallen fruit lying in the grass and weeds.

The luscious, golden apricots literally exploded with rich juice between my lips. Here, standing out in the wide sweep of the open range, was a solitary tree unattended by any man. It had not been fertilized, had never been pruned, and had never had any chemical sprays upon its blossoms or branches. This was pristine, pure, perfect fruit distilled from wild sod, warm sunlight, and sparse rainfall in this untamed site.

For me, as a rather rough mountain man, this was a moment of supreme satisfaction, of pure pleasure, and of deep delight. For in a special sense I was savoring one of those "beautiful bonuses" my Father so often imparts to my life.

Finding these firstfruits in such a simple but joyous way is in reality a mini-miracle bestowed with grace and generosity by my Father's gentle hand. I am not a man to look for sensational or spectacular demonstrations of divine power. A taste of wild apricots on a remote range is enough.

We pushed on further into the hills. A wild, as yet untamed, river cut its winding course between the rugged ranges. We followed its valley and came to a small, cute log cabin. Beside it stood a magnificent apricot tree laden with rich, red fruit.

A line of fresh laundry blew in the breeze. So I was sure someone was home. Sure enough, the lady of the little log cabin was up in the branches of a huge cherry tree gleaning the last of this year's black cherry crop. She was an affable soul, all smiles, with dancing eyes.

Quickly she came down from her perch and greeted us warmly. The fact was, her laden apricot tree was grafted to several varieties of which the brilliant red fruit were peachcots, a brand new fruit to us. Only a few of the first ripe fruits had fallen. Of these only a few were fit to gather for her grandchildren. The rest were left as a banquet for the deer.

With the gracious geniality so typical of frontier folk, she pressed us to come into her compact cabin. Full of joy, she poured us each a glass of cool, clear water and served us each a delicious homemade cookie just drawn from her oven.

Very quickly we discovered that lovely spirit of goodwill which draws our Father's children together in the lovely bonds of His family. We were there only a few minutes, for she was a busy lady, but they were memorable moments of intense joy, like jewels spilled into this still and gentle morning.

We parted as friends who had known each other for much,

much longer than time could tell. I presume that is what it will be like in the next life when all of us who truly love our beloved Friend and Lord, Christ Himself, meet for the first time in the wondrous warmth of His presence.

Just as we were leaving, we exchanged names, almost as an afterthought. Then, in a supreme gesture of goodwill, she gathered up the apricots and peachcots, first fallen from her tree, and pressed them upon us with pure pleasure shining in her eyes.

We came home singing. What a memorable morning! Firstfruits.

Firstfruits!

Building Soil

Often in this little book reference has been made to the rather rugged, rocky ridge on which we live. It is indeed a superb spot for sweeping views over the lake below us and for wide vistas across the encircling mountain ranges. But it is tough terrain in which to try to grow a garden.

The first year we came here a generous couple who loved gardening and owned a rather large estate offered to let me use part of their land. It was deep, rich soil with automatic sprinklers installed, so growing a beautiful crop of vegetables was assured.

There was one great drawback. It was miles from home, and tending the spot demanded long drives and constant care. Still I looked at my stony, sun-blasted ridge and wondered, wondered, wondered if we could somehow work miracles on our hill in some simple way.

I am not a "modern man" who uses large sums of money, roaring machines, and human ingenuity to impose my will on the world. I could have brought in contractors to build retaining walls of concrete and brick. Tons and tons of fill and topsoil could have been hauled in from afar. The resulting terraces could have been tilled and tended with power tillers, roaring mowers and chemical weed control. None of that nonsense appealed to my primitive instincts.

Surely there must be a better way, a simple way, a sure gentle way to just build some soil in this challenging spot—without all the fuss, all the ferocious fanfare, or all the engine fumes of modern man.

Last winter during a blinding blizzard with the north wind moaning at the windows, I decided at any cost to try a humble, simple strategy to create some new soil in nature's own quiet way. All it involved was collecting up the grass clippings that my neighbors were sending off to the landfill and spreading them in a deep mulch over the rocky, weedy ground. I called the grass I gathered and used this way "green gold."

The name was appropriate in more ways than one. First and foremost it was because very quickly the deep, thick blanket of lawn clippings literally smothered all the noxious weeds. This in itself saved me endless summer labor. Secondly, the deep, green mulch soon turned to gold under the sun, providing a dense carpet of organic material that retained all the moisture that fell upon it. Thirdly, it surprised me to see that virtually no wind-blown seeds could take root in this protective cover.

Almost in trembling faith I staked out a special patch in which to plant my garden. There would be no digging, no spading, no disturbance of the ground, no hoeing, and no weeding. I simply opened the mulch enough to place the seed on the thin soil, covered it gently with the clippings—*then waited!*

The results defy description. Already this season from that stony spot we have harvested peas, onions, radishes, potatoes, and beans. There are no signs of any diseases in the crops. They are lush, rich, and bountiful beyond belief. Best of all, wherever I move the mulch I find healthy, active, thick-bodied earthworms converting the abundance of organic matter into fertile, new soil.

Are you surprised I call this great adventure in gardening *green gold?* Like so many experiments in life, it has been the simple way, the ordinary use of ordinary things, the humble harmony of working in company with our Father's arrangements of the earth that have produced such astonishing results.

So often as I stand alone in the garden and look at its green glory, I ponder if this is not after all precisely how Christ wants us to live all of life—in simplicity, in quietness, and in gentle harmony with His will for us. We are too often caught up in grandiose strategies, mind-boggling technology, and so-called human skills. No wonder we go, go, go until we drop!

"Oh, my Father, my Friend, my Fellow Companion, please, just spread the mantle of your *gracious green glory (Your own gentle presence)* over the stormy ground of my stony soul . . . *to become the garden of Your care.*"

Windstorm

Two days in succession the ferocious winds roared through our valley like lions setting out to kill. The growling gusts tugged at trees, broke off branches, stripped shrubs, and bent the blasted vegetation down to the ground.

It would have been an alarming storm if our house had not been built on solid rock, anchored to the very bedrock of the ridge with massive walls of reinforced concrete. In dismay we watched a neighbor's shed torn off its foundation and flung all askew with the door blown open.

It was almost as if there was a threat of death in the fierce fury of the windstorm. Plants shriveled and withered under its hot breath. The green lawns and verdant ground cover stood stark and stressed, drained of moisture, in the wild wind that would and could turn them brown in hours.

I wondered if all the labor, all the love, and all the long hours of gentle care that had been lavished in the garden would be blown to bits, beaten to nothing by the desert blow! Life is just like that at times. The labor, the love, and the longing care we have poured out freely for other people suddenly seems to come to nothing. It is as if the very breath of death descends upon the scene. The situation is scarred, strained, stressed, and sad.

Has it all been for naught?
Was it really wasted work, wasted time, and wasted love?
Hard questions under the harsh windstorm of reality
No, no, a thousand times NO!
Nothing done in care and compassion is in vain.

Suddenly last night, just as darkness descended over our drought stricken scene, random raindrops started to spatter on the windows. Soon they increased to a steady, warm shower. It persisted all night, drawn by the wind from the far reaches of the brooding Pacific. At dawn the whole world was still and soft and shining with fresh life. All was green again!

Our Father arranges for great good to come out of every experience.
Out of apparent disaster He can bring deep delight.
He can use a windstorm to work wonders under His command.

Diamonds for the Day

Each day is sprinkled with diamonds of great worth.
But we must look for them!
They are available to anyone who takes the time—the
trouble—the thought to search seriously.
Like the flashing gemstones of jewelry they are
found only by those with eyes to see and hearts
to seize.

A t dawn, as is my custom every morning, I went outside
to stand softly in the garden. After the ferocious winds
and erratic thunderstorms of the previous night, all
was still. Not a leaf or blade of grass moved in the intense
silence. Instead, each was adorned with a flashing, shining gem
of moisture suspended from its slender, green growth.
Ten million diamonds of dew decorated my world.
What gorgeous gifts! Not processed and shaped by the
hand of man or the technology of his industry, but rather crafted
to perfection by the principles and powers of the natural physical realm ordained by God my Father.
This incredible, shining display of diamonds in my day had
been lavished on my life in love from His generous hands. In
awe and gratitude I stood in silence giving thanks.

At breakfast, in our cute kitchen nook, warm rays from the morning sun spilled their golden warmth across the table. Somehow, any day that started this way was precious. The glowing light painted a stunning picture before my eyes.

A kind neighbor often shares her gorgeous roses with us. Their beauty is more than doubled as their soft petals greet the day and grow mellow in the low light. They glow and pulse with perfection as if shaped from the most expensive porcelain. Some days they almost take my breath away with their incandescent beauty.

The same is apparent for the bowls of fresh fruit on the breakfast table. Bananas, oranges, grapes, apricots, or apples each shine in the sun. Reflecting its golden glow, they paint pictures of pure pleasure.

Each is a diamond in this day to delight the eye.

I decided to set aside all the demands of this day. It was a deliberate act of will. A dozen other duties could have claimed my attention. But I was determined to search for diamonds, precious moments, special memories, to store in the vault of my memory. No man could ever steal them from this secret storehouse. So I headed for the beckoning hills.

Just a few minutes from my home I turned off onto a rough country road. Its surface sparkled in the sun, each particle of gravel, stone, and sand had been washed clean by the storm. My tracks were the first imprint on it for this memorable morning.

Suddenly, swiftly, with staccato wing beats, scores and scores and scores of desert doves rose from the roadway. The smooth, sleek, gray-backed birds were everywhere. Normally they are only seen here in rather shy and solitary pairs. This day their flocks filled the air. For me this was a first.

Obviously, the swift-winged wanderers of the winds were gathering gravel on the verges of the road. And also they were feeding heartily on the rich abundance of ripened grass seeds all along the edges.

I have always loved the low notes of the wild doves that drift across our dry desert rangeland. I once owned a dramatic mount of a pair of doves posed on a gnarled piece of wild juniper wood.

Today scores of doves had become diamonds in my day.

I parked the car in the safety of the sagebrush on a wide bench above the valley. Just as I stepped out to inhale the sweet fragrance of the gray sage, a magnificent mule deer doe threw up her head to test the air and see who had stepped into her world.

She was adorned in her conspicuous, reddish summer coat. I knew at once by her nervous actions that she had a fawn hidden in the brush nearby. Momentarily, she monitored my soft movements. Her extended ears, like a couple of sensitive radar antenna, tracked me carefully. Then with gentle grace and flowing muscles she bounded away to pick up her baby and be gone.

I had seen it all before in my mountain days. Still it thrilled me. *Another diamond added to the memory of this morning.*

Relaxed, contented in spirit, and at one with my wilderness world, I wandered softly over the slopes and meadows of the hills. Never in more than fifty years of roaming this rangeland had I seen such a luxuriant growth of grass. It was a deep delight to see the hills swathed in such a gorgeous ground cover. For all the wild ones there would be an abundance of feed this fall and winter. Mountain sheep, mule deer, whitetails, marmots, rabbits, yes even mice and moles would revel in the banquet prepared for them by the summer showers.

So many seasons I had seen these slopes stressed and scarred by summer heat. The soil was parched and panting for relief. The vegetation was sparse and scarce. But this year was different. *This day sparkled with the diamond of quiet joy.*

I laid down on a giant outcrop of granite covered in moss. Stretched in the soft morning sun, I sensed the sweet, plaintive notes of a pair of meadowlarks flowing over me. Always, always, always their song has spelled out the special spell of wild places, wild grasslands, and wild spaces. It was no different today, for I never saw another soul. Just the wild song from the tip of a tall pine, *another diamond of pure delight.*

As the morning moved on, a fresh, clean, cool, energizing breeze began to blow across the rugged, upland range. The air was so delicious, so stimulating, it stirred every fiber in my body. Standing on tiptoe in the sun I opened my lungs fully, expanding my chest to inhale great drafts of the oxygen charged air.

It was like an elixir of great worth, energizing, quickening, and renewing every part of my being. Audibly, unashamedly, and joyously I lifted my voice, my spirit, and my soul to give Christ, my Lord, thanks for still *another unforgettable diamond in this day*.

There is a serene secret in all of this.

> *Relish this moment: Cherish this day.*
> *Then yesterday becomes a diamond of delight.*
> *And tomorrow can be a treasure trove of hope.*

The Gift of Grass

The ancients called grass *"The Great Healer."*
It is a beautiful title well deserved.
For the planet would indeed be a bleak place without it.

I have been in the regions of the earth where because of severe desert conditions, lack of rain and perpetual drought, grass simply could not strike root or survive. I have also worked and labored and struggled to restore wasted, ravaged land, turned to desert waste, by the greedy grasping hands of careless men.

And always it was grass that was *"The Great Healer."*

Grass has the incredible capacity to cover over the ragged scars and dreadful damage we do to the earth. It steals softly over the barren soil we so often abuse with our giant machines and roaring equipment that tear up the terrain.

Every new housing development, every new highway, and every new commercial expansion in the name of so-called "progress" exacts deep wounds of desolation on the land. And it is only by turning to grass and trees and shrubs that we can hope to be saved from becoming an utterly brutal society.

As it is, we have contrived our ghastly ghettoes in our giant metropolitan centers that are sterile settings for crime, violence, and mindless mayhem. The one redeeming feature in all the desolation of our drastic designs is the co-called "green spaces." We hope some open spaces where grass can grow, where children can play and run in the sun, and where the elderly can rest on the cool green sward may just help to save our society from utter savagery.

These impressions and scores of others surge through my soul as I set the sprinklers on my lawns all summer long. I raise my spirit in heartfelt thanks for the cool, green carpet of grass that freshens the air around my home. This green sward is a gathering ground for the birds, for the bees, and for the deer that relish its gentle environment and find quiet peace in this place of rest.

But my moments of reflection go far, far beyond the blades of grass that flourish with the fresh water falling upon them. They go beyond the ever deepening layer of soil produced by the decaying litter of grass clippings left behind by the sharp-edged mower. They go beyond the pure pleasure of proving a lovely piece of lawn in a desert world of sagebrush and grease-wood and burning summer sun.

For in this grass I perceive a precious gift for all of us from the gentle, generous, and gracious hand of my Father. It is He who first conceived of such a lovely covering for the land. But beyond that the grass provides a bounty of benefits for men and birds, bees and insects, and livestock and wildlife. Each of us in our own way are blessed by its abundance.

Two nights ago I was hand watering a small triangle of grass that struggles to survive on a barren gravel patch beside our driveway. Slowly but steadily it has gradually improved across the years. Constant care and loving husbandry have turned the spot from a waste weed patch into an emerald lawn of beauty to the eye.

Suddenly the startling thought surged into my spirit with profound impact. *That is exactly what the grace of God does amid the desolation of life. His grace is the generous, precious gift of His presence.*

We so often hear and sing that glorious old melody "Amaz-ing Grace." Like grass we are the ones who benefit from its presence in our world, in our lives, and in our souls. It comes to us in gracious abundance as a gift from our God. Yet we take it so much for granted, so much abused, and so much trod upon without much thought or gratitude.

As with grass, so with God's grace, it is the great healer that covers all our wrongs, our torn up lives, and our tired tempestuous spirits. What a glorious gift from above to save our languishing souls.

Thank you, Father, for grass!
Thank you, Father, for Your grace!

Fallen Feathers

O n my desk, mounted handsomely beneath my work lamp, stand a pair of California quail. They are amongst my favorites of the wild bird species in this upland realm. From our great windows overlooking the valley we watch their movements with never ending fascination-—and yes, sometimes trepidation. For they must survive the fierce predation of hawks, coyotes, cats, and dogs.

Yesterday I went to gather another bountiful crop of tomatoes from the garden. To my dismay, part of the potato patch was littered with the scattered, fallen feathers of a quail. The beautiful bird had fallen prey to the stealthy, wild, black cat that stalks the covey relentlessly.

The cat, elusive as a puff of dark smoke, has hunted these hills for years. Every attempt to trap the fierce hunter has failed. Sharp-eyed, swift-clawed, and agile as a flash of fury the stalker takes a steady toll of the birds that seem so heedless of its presence.

The fallen feathers tell their own grim tale of careless quail wandering at will into the shrubbery where they have seen others of their kind slaughtered by the swift hunter. We often stand at the windows with bated breath and racing pulse wondering why the quail choose again and again to put themselves in harm's way.

There is an explosive pounce, the raking of claws, the sharp crunch of teeth, torn flesh, and sudden death! Then we are shot through with sorrow.

I stood and looked longingly at the fallen feathers. Sad. Then in a flash, sudden, acute, and intense illumination came to my inner consciousness. It was like a stabbing pain.

We human beings are exactly the same! In our folly, in our stupid wilfullness, and in our careless choices, we put ourselves in harm's way.

Again and again we have seen others fall prey to our adversary. Yet somehow in our cocky self-assurance we risk dangerous places and dare destructive encounters. Always, always, our pride precedes our awful fall.

Cleansing

Unlike many of the homes around us, we do not have any sort of underground watering system or even drip irrigation. For my trees, shrubs, lawns, and garden to survive I simply have to do the watering by hand or move the sprinklers from place to place as the heat of the season demands.

This calls for careful attention, but the quiet interludes give time to think long thoughts, and most joyfully keep me in close contact with all the growing vegetation under my care. Not only does the flow of water falling on foliage refresh the plants and trees and shrubs, but also cleanses them continually.

There is a supremely satisfying sensation of seeing the dust, the insects, the spider webs, and the clinging pollen swept away from the leaves, the needles, the fruit, and blossoms in my care. In an instant the grime is gone and the vegetation sparkles clean and bright and shining in the morning sunlight. Across the years the plant growth cleansed this way shows wholesome vigor, a surprising freedom from duress, and above all virtually no insect damage.

My neighbors wage a constant war with various *infestations*. They hire chemical companies to come in with their high powered sprays and deadly pesticides. None of these pollute the plants or trees around our home. Just the cleansing stream of regular washing with water provides us with all the protection we need. Yesterday I stood quietly in the morning sun and reflected calmly on this theme. The spray from the hose in my hand shone silver in the bright light. The cleansing stream made all things fresh and new and fit.

No wonder our Father, in His wondrous Word, assures us likewise that we need the constant cleansing of His life, His love, and His Word. It is an on-going process. Continually we are besmirched, soiled, stained, and defiled by our environment.

But to maintain us in strength, in vigor, in wholeness, and in well-being He comes to us in kindness, care, and compassion. He comes to cleanse, and He comes to make us anew this day. His name is at stake in us.

Autumn Glory

Yesterday it came, though in unusual sequence, the gentle glory of fall . . . touching all of life with its abundant grace . . . a cluster of precious moments combined in a simple autumn day.

At dawn I stood at the open window facing north along the silver lake. Cool arctic air flowed around my face. It came with vigor; it came strongly; it came silently. But I knew at once that the heat of the summer was past. The hot desert winds were done. So I relished the moment, giving thanks for the release.

An hour later Ursula and I were stirred suddenly by the wild, haunting cries of scores of Canada geese lifting off the lake. We rushed to the kitchen nook to watch the strong-winged birds launch themselves into the chill air, their upward rush carrying them past our sun decks with wild abandon. They too could sense fall in the air, with its powerful urge to send them south.

Pure joy, pure adventure, pure power.

Then, just as we concluded our morning devotions, I heard the ringing challenge of a bald-headed eagle drift down out of the clouds. In a quick search of the sky I soon spotted not just one eagle, but three of the great, handsome birds soaring over the hills behind our home. Two were adults in fresh full plumage. The third was a juvenile still garbed in gray.

They soared easily in giant spirals, cutting circles in the heavy cloud cover. Almost exactly a year ago I had been witness to a tremendous aerial duel right over our hill between a huge bald eagle and a defiant osprey. It went on and on. The slim-winged osprey appeared more agile and athletic in full flight. But the rapier beak and great outstretched claws of the bald eagle kept his attacker at bay. Finally, completely exhausted, both birds broke off the battle.

But yesterday the eagles had the sky to themselves.

Finally, all three birds settled down on the bare branches of an old fir snag within rifle shot of our front door. What a superb sight and a sure sign they too were preparing for the long flight south.

Already it had been a bountiful, beautiful day. But it was far from done. Autumn's glory was spilling out around us, filling our cup of thanksgiving with overflowing abundance.

In the nearby village an elderly friend happened to park next to my car. He waited for me to come back. We chatted a few moments; then he expressed a desire to come over and see my luxuriant clover and incredible garden growing on broken rock and shale. He and his son were both outstanding landscape gardeners.

He followed me home in joy. But that joy turned to pure pleasure when his eyes fell on the luxuriant growth all around our home. "BEAUTIFUL—BEAUTIFUL—BEAUTIFUL!" he burst out. "Utterly unbelievable!"

We shared a cup of coffee and crackers and cheese, while we chatted about plants and trees and flowers and fruit. Yes, yes, all of it part of autumn's glory. There was a sparkle in his eyes and warmth in his soul when he headed for home—in ours as well.

Already I had been into the garden to gather a ripe abundance of red tomatoes and green beans. All of them so perfect, without blemishes, rich in flavor, even though grown on such stony ground, nourished by the thick mulch of mown grass and earthworm casts.

Where but one year ago there had been only weeds and waste, barren ground—now a garden grew in green glory. The

peas, the radishes, the flowers, the beans, the onions, and the tomatoes that came from that spot had nourished not only us, but our friends and neighbors as well.

Always, always there was an abundance. A joyous harvest!

"Oh, Father, may the little garden of my soul be the same!"

Still this memorable day had a special surprise in store for us. Ursula and I had just prepared ourselves to drive into town to call on a dear fellow in the hospital. We were going in deep concern, for he had suffered a massive stroke. He was half paralyzed, unable to even swallow a sip of cool water. We had sat by his bed in anguish; yes, and in our home we wept, hot, scalding tears over his suffering. We had cried out in agony for Christ to intercede on his behalf. Long, long before dawn I had pleaded that there would be some respite.

Then just as we were ready to leave the house the phone rang. I reached for it wondering what message it might bring. It was the dear man's wife. She was buoyant with good news. That very morning he had begun to swallow. She herself had been able to give him his first drink of cool, clear water after four weeks of absolute agony.

"Thank you, Father! Thank you, Father!" we cried aloud. He had turned the corner! Soon there would follow some nourishing, warm, homemade chicken broth, then other wholesome foods to restore his strength. Already we had offered to do this as soon as he was able to swallow.

In youthful glee, Ursula and I waved the "thumbs up" sign of triumph to each other. Things were turning around. The doctors were supplying him with a special bed, a special chair, and special therapy to restore his mobility. Hope sprang anew. Christ had touched his life. He had touched all those who cared for him. He had touched us!

This was a day of autumn glory.
This was a day of abundant joy.
This was a day of thanks and calm trust in Christ.
No wonder we call this the season of Thanksgiving.

It is a time to celebrate wild birds on wing, lovely bountiful harvests from the land, and joyous delight in seeing our Father's hand at work in the world.

And out of our thanks great pleasure comes to Him, who gives us autumn glory.

Moment of Majesty

D awn was breathtaking . . . bright with both the moon set in the west and intense with the sunrise in the east. Seldom, seldom does one see such a spectacle in the skies.

It had been the night of full moon. All the earth lay still, silent, and silver under the mystery of its mellow light. As the hours passed, the glowing orb moved steadily across the night sky until just at daybreak its majesty stood serene above the western mountain ranges. Its glowing, reflected rays flooded the windows of my study, filling the room with brightness.

Added to all of this was a broken cloud cover scattered over the rocky ridges. Steadily, the cumulus formations turned from white to pale pink then pulsing crimson, ignited by the rising sun over the eastern skyline.

Never, never, in all my life had I seen such an unusual moonset. The golden orb of the harvest moon stood in majesty surrounded by radiant robes of scarlet and crimson clouds. It was not only a moment of majesty, but also a moment never to be forgotten!

In that shining instant there came to my soul, my spirit, my spiritual awareness an acute sense of the very presence of the eternal Spirit of God Himself. In this moment of majesty I knew again something of the grandeur of the Most High, something of the supreme glory of Christ the Creator who sustains all things by the Word of His mouth and something of the power of His presence in all the universe.

In awe, wonder, and humility I was bowed before Him, in whom I live and move and have my very being.

I was still, and in that stillness I knew God in His majesty, His magnificence, and His most high honor.

The whole earth is filled with His glory for those of us with eyes to see, ears to hear, and spirits sensitive for His own. In that moment a common man was reassured again and again—

"Oh, my Father, Your faithfulness is forever: Oh, Christ, my Friend, Your mercies are new every morning!"